German Easy Reader

Super 500

Brian Smith

This is a work of fiction. Names, characters, businesses, places, events and incidents are either the products of the author's imagination or used in a fictitious manner. Any resemblance to actual persons, living or dead, or actual events is purely coincidental.

Introduction

This easy reader is based on the 500 most common words in German. Knowing these will enable you to understand 80% of average German texts. The aim of this book is to introduce these words and practise using them along with the three most common tenses and sentence structures until you have a very solid foundation and can move on to more challenging aspects of German with confidence.

In each chapter you will find the original German text side by side with an English translation. The purpose of the translation is to help you better understand the German text, so the English version follows the German original closely. This makes the English sound peculiar at times but it serves its purpose.

All new words are introduced with an English translation in the text. This makes it easier to read the text without having to go back and forth between pages to check the meaning. Please note that the English translations give the meaning used in the text. For full information you should consult a dictionary.

You will also find numerous pictures to illustrate new words.
There are many verb tables that show you how to conjugate new verbs correctly.

You may notice as you read through the book that words and sentence structures such as common statements, questions and answers are repeated many times with only slight variations. This constant repetition will enable you to internalize basic German syntax. Once it has become second nature to you, it will be much easier to expand your vocabulary without having to give much thought to grammar and syntax.

To help you with the pronunciation an MP3 recording of the German text in each unit is available for free at

www.briansmith.de

Go to 'BOOKS' and select 'German Easy Reader'.

To get the most out of this book it would be a good idea to read each chapter a few times on different days and, if you can, listen to the recording while reading. Nature has pre-programmed the human brain to remember things it sees and hears frequently, so repetition is the key to successful language learning.
If you find it easy to understand everything, congratulations. If not, don't worry. Go on to the next chapter and come back to earlier chapters after a few days. You will find that it has become much easier.
And finally, remember that this is a special kind of reader. It was designed to help you learn the most frequent vocabulary and grammatical structures without having to study vocabulary lists or doing grammar exercises. So don't rush through it. Take your time, relax, and improve your German the easy way.

Good luck and have fun!

Inhaltsverzeichnis / Contents

Über den Autor / About the author

Brian Smith was born in Germany in 1972. Son of a German mother and an English father he grew up having both German and English as his native languages. He grew up and completed his education in Germany. In 1995 he moved to Hong Kong where he spent twenty years teaching English and German. He has also learned several languages including French, Latin and Cantonese.

His extensive teaching experience in two different languages to people from various countries and his own experience in successfully learning foreign languages have given him a unique insight about the best ways to help learners make progress.

Brian Smith wurde 1972 in Deutschland geboren. Als Sohn einer deutschen Mutter und eines englischen Vaters ist er mit sowohl Deutsch als auch Englisch als Muttersprachen aufgewachsen. Er ist in Deutschland aufgewachsen und hat dort seine Bildung abgeschlossen. 1995 ist er nach Hong Kong gezogen, wo er zwanzig Jahre lang Englisch und Deutsch unterrichtet hat. Er hat auch mehrere Sprachen gelernt, darunter Französisch, Latein und Kantonesisch.

Dank seiner großen Erfahrung Menschen verschiedener Länder Sprachen beizubringen, und seiner eigenen Erfahrung im Lernen von Fremdsprachen hat er ein einzigartiges Verständniss davon, wie man jemandem der eine Fremdsprache lernt am besten helfen kann.

Erstes Kapitel

der Junge
the boy

der Mann
the man

das Mädchen
the girl

die Frau
the woman

Peter ist ein Junge. Marie ist ein Mädchen. Frau Schmidt ist eine Frau. Herr Schmidt ist ein Mann.	Peter is a boy. Marie is a girl. Mrs. Schmidt is a woman. Mr. Schmidt is a man.

das Kind - **the child**

die Mutter - **the mother**

die Kinder - **the children**

der Vater - **the father**

Peter ist ein Kind und Marie ist ein Kind. Peter und Marie sind Kinder. Frau Schmidt ist die Mutter von Peter und Marie. Herr Schmidt ist der Vater.	Peter is a child and Marie is a child. Peter and Marie are children. Mrs. Schmidt is the mother of Peter and Marie. Mr. Schmidt is the father.

heißt - **is called**

Schwester - **sister**

ihr/ihre - **her**

Bruder - **brother**

sein/seine - **his**

Ein Kind heißt Marie. Ihre Mutter heißt Frau Schmidt.
Ein Kind heißt Peter. Sein Vater heißt Herr Schmidt.
Peter hat eine Schwester. Seine Schwester heißt Marie.
Marie hat einen Bruder. Ihr Bruder heißt Peter.

wie - **how**	nein - **no**
von - **of**	ja - **yes**

Wie heißt der Bruder von Marie? Ihr Bruder heißt Peter.
Wie heißt die Schwester von Peter? Seine Schwester heißt Marie.
Wie heißt der Vater von Marie? Ihr Vater heißt Herr Schmidt.
Wie heißt die Mutter von Peter? Seine Mutter heißt Frau Schmidt.
Ist Frau Schmidt ein Mädchen? Nein. Frau Schmidt ist eine Frau.
Ist Herr Schmidt ein Junge? Nein. Herr Schmidt ist ein Mann.
Ist Peter ein Junge? Ja. Peter ist ein Junge.
Ist Marie ein Mädchen? Ja. Marie ist ein Mädchen.

Eltern - **parents**	die Leute - **people**
heißen - **are called**	der Freund - **friend**
Familie - **family**	der Hund - **dog**

Herr und Frau Schmidt sind die Eltern von Marie und Peter.
Peter und Marie sind Kinder. Ihre Eltern sind Herr und Frau Schmidt.
Wie heißen die Eltern von Peter und Marie? Ihre Eltern heißen Herr Schmidt und Frau Schmidt.
Die Eltern und die Kinder sind eine Familie. In der Familie sind ein Mann, eine Frau, ein Junge und ein Mädchen. Es sind vier Leute in der Familie.

One child is called Marie. Her mother is called Mrs. Schmidt.
One child is called Peter. His father is called Mr. Schmidt.
Peter has a sister. His sister is called Marie.
Marie has a brother. Her brother is called Peter.

What is Marie's brother called? Her brother is called Peter.
What is Peter's sister called? His sister is called Marie.

What is Marie's father called? Her father is called Mr.
Schmidt. What is Peter's mother called? His mother is called
Mrs. Schmidt.
Is Mrs. Schmidt a girl? No. Mrs. Schmidt is a woman.

Is Mr. Schmidt a boy? No. Mr. Schmidt is a man.
Is Peter a boy? Yes. Peter is a boy.
Is Marie a girl? Yes. Marie is a girl.

> **Note**: In German 'Freund' refers to a male friend, while
> 'Freundin' refers to a female friend.

Mr. and Mrs. Schmidt are the parents of Marie and Peter.
Peter and Marie are children. Their parents are Mr. and Mrs.
Schmidt
What are the parents of Peter and Marie called? Their parents
are called Mr. and Mrs. Schmidt.
The parents and the children are a family. In the family there
is a man, a woman, a boy and a girl. There are four people in
the family.

Rex gehört zur Familie.
Ist Rex ein Junge? Nein.
Ist Rex ein Mädchen? Nein.

 **ein Hund**

Ist Rex eine Frau? Nein.
Ist Rex ein Hund? Ja. Rex ist ein Hund.
Die Familie hat einen Hund. Wie heißt der Hund? Der Hund heißt Rex.
Die Kinder lieben Rex. Rex ist ihr Freund.
Der Hund liebt die Kinder. Sie sind seine Freunde.
Lieben Herr und Frau Schmidt den Hund? Ja, sie lieben den Hund. Der Hund ist ihr Freund.
Sind Herr und Frau Schmidt die Eltern von Rex? Nein, sie sind die Eltern von Marie und Peter.

1 – eins
2 – zwei
3 – drei
4 – vier
5 – fünf
6 – sechs
7 – sieben
8 – acht
9 – neun
10 – zehn

Rex belongs to the family.
Is Rex a boy? No.
Is Rex a girl? No.

zwei Hunde

Is Rex a woman? No.
Is Rex a dog? Yes. Rex is a dog.
The family has a dog. What is the dog called? The dog is called Rex.
The children love Rex. Rex is their friend.
The dog loves the children. They are his friends.
Do Mr. and Mrs. Schmidt love the dog? Yes, they love the dog. The dog is their friend.
Are Mr. and Mrs. Schmidt the parents of Rex? No, they are the parents of Marie and Peter.

ein Mann	zwei Männer
eine Frau	drei Frauen
ein Mädchen	vier Mädchen
ein Junge	fünf Jungen
ein Hund	sechs Hunde
ein Kind	sieben Kinder
eine Familie	acht Familien
ein Freund	neun Freunde
eine Freundin	zehn Freundinnen

11

Was sagen sie?

Peter: „Ich heiße Peter. Ich bin ein Junge. Meine Schwester heißt Marie. Wir haben einen Hund. Mein Hund heißt Rex."

Marie: „Ich heiße Marie und mein Bruder heißt Peter. Ich bin ein Mädchen. Wir haben einen Hund, der Rex heißt. Wir lieben unseren Hund."

Frau Schmidt: „Ich bin Frau Schmidt. Ich habe zwei Kinder, ein Mädchen und einen Jungen. Sie heißen Marie und Peter."

Herr Schmidt: „Ich bin Herr Schmidt. In meiner Familie sind vier Leute und ein Hund. Ich habe eine Frau und zwei Kinder."

Peter und Marie: „Wir lieben unsere Eltern und unsere Eltern lieben uns."

alt – **old**   nicht - **not**
jung – **young**

Wie alt ist der Hund? Der Hund ist ein Jahr alt. Er ist jung.
Wie alt ist das Mädchen? Marie ist sieben Jahre alt. Sie ist jung.
Wie alt ist der Junge? Peter ist acht Jahre alt. Er ist jung.
Wie alt sind die Eltern? Sie sind nicht jung. Sie sind alt.
Sind die Eltern jung? Nein. Sie sind alt.
Sind die Kinder jung? Ja. Sie sind jung.
Ist der Hund alt? Nein. Der Hund ist jung.

Peter: „Marie, bist du alt?"
Marie: „Nein, ich bin nicht alt. Ich bin jung."
Peter: „Ist unser Vater jung?"

What are they saying?

Peter: "I'm called Peter. I'm a boy. My sister is called Marie. We have a dog. My dog is called Rex."

Marie: "I'm called Marie and my brother is called Peter. I'm a girl. We have a dog called Rex. We love our dog.

Mrs. Schmidt: "I am Mrs. Schmidt. I have two children, a girl and a boy. They are called Marie and Peter."

Mr. Schmidt: "I am Mr. Schmidt. In my family there are four people and a dog. I have a wife and two children."

Peter and Marie: "We love our parents and our parents love us."

How old is the dog? The dog is one year old. It is young.
How old is the girl? Marie is seven years old. She is young.

How old is the boy? Peter is eight years old. He is young.
How old are the parents? They are not young. They are old.
Are the parents young? No. They are old.
Are the children young? Yes. They are young.
Is the dog old? No. The dog is young.

Peter: "Marie, are you old?"
Marie: "No, I'm not old. I'm young."
Peter. "Is our father young?"

Marie: „Nein, er ist nicht jung. Er ist alt."
Peter: „Ist der Hund alt?"
Marie: „Nein, er ist nicht alt. Er ist jung."

 **ein alter Mann**

 **ein junger Mann**

Marie: "No, he isn't young. He's old."
Peter: "Is the dog old?"
Marie: "No, it isn't old. It's young."

zwei alte Männer

zwei junge Männer

Zweites Kapitel

der Ball – **ball**
das Bett – **bed**

spielen – **play**
schlafen - **sleep**

Der Hund spielt mit einem Ball. Die Kinder spielen mit dem Hund. Rex ist ihr Freund. Spielen die Eltern mit dem Ball? Nein, sie spielen nicht mit dem Ball. Die Eltern sind im Bett und schlafen.
Schlafen die Kinder? Nein, sie schlafen nicht und der Hund schläft nicht. Sie spielen mit dem Ball.

was - **what**
machen - **do**
im – **in the**

der Garten - **garden**
die Straße - **road, street**
auf – **on the**

Was machen die Eltern? Sie schlafen im Bett.
Was machen die Kinder? Sie spielen mit dem Hund.
Was macht der Hund? Er spielt mit dem Ball.
Spielt der Hund auf der Straße? Nein, der Hund spielt nicht auf der Straße. Er spielt im Garten.
Schlafen die Eltern im Garten? Nein, sie schlafen im Bett.
Was macht Peter? Er spielt mit dem Hund im Garten.
Was macht Marie? Sie spielt im Garten.
Die Kinder und der Hund spielen im Garten. Sie spielen nicht auf der Straße.

wo - **where**
wir - **we**

da - **there**
liegen - **lie** (in bed)

Wo ist der Vater? Der Vater liegt im Bett.
Liegt die Mutter im Garten? Nein, sie liegt nicht im Garten. Sie liegt im Bett. Die Eltern liegen im Bett.

Second Chapter

eine Straße – zwei Straßen

The dog is playing with a ball. The children are playing with the dog. Rex is their friend. Are the parents playing with the ball? No, they aren't playing with the ball. The parents are in bed sleeping.
Are the children sleeping? No, they aren't sleeping and the dog isn't sleeping. They are playing with the ball.

ich spiele	wir spielen
du spielst	ihr spielt
er, sie, es spielt	sie spielen

What are the parents doing? They are sleeping in bed.
What are the children doing? They're playing with the dog.
What's the dog doing? It's playing with the ball.
Is the dog playing on the road? No, the dog isn't playing on the road. It's playing in the garden.
Are the parents sleeping in the garden? No, they're sleeping in bed. What's Peter doing? He's playing with the dog in the garden. What's Marie doing? She's playing in the garden.
The children and the dog are playing in the garden. They aren't playing on the road.

Where is the father? Father is lying in bed.
Is mother lying in the garden? No, she isn't lying in the garden. She's lying in bed. The parents are lying in bed.

17

Wo ist der Hund? Der Hund ist im Garten, er ist nicht auf der Straße.
Wo sind die Kinder? Sie sind im Garten.

gut - **good**	die Angst - **fear**
sehr - **very**	rufen - **call**
gehen – **go, walk**	

er hat Angst	**he is afraid**

 **die Straße**

Peter: „Wo ist der Ball?"
Marie: „Da ist der Ball. Der Hund hat den Ball."
Peter: „Der Hund ist nicht im Garten. Wo ist der Hund?"
Marie: „Der Hund ist auf der Straße."
Peter: „Das ist nicht gut. Ich habe Angst."
Marie ruft den Hund.
Der Hund geht in den Garten. Er ist nicht auf der Straße.
Peter: „Sehr gut, der Hund ist im Garten."

kommen - **come**	hier - **here**
der Baum - **tree**	der Vogel - **bird**

Die Mutter kommt in den Garten. Sie liegt nicht im Bett und sie schläft nicht.
Frau Schmidt: „Wo ist der Hund?"
Kinder: „Er ist hier. Wir spielen mit dem Hund."
Frau Schmidt: „Wo ist euer Ball?"

Where is the dog? The dog is in the garden, it isn't on the road.
Where are the children? They're in the garden.

 **ein Auto ist auf der Straße**

Peter: "Where's the ball?"
Marie: "There is the ball. The dog has the ball."
Peter: "The dog isn't in the garden. Where is the dog?"
Marie: "The dog is on the road."
Peter: "That's not good. I'm worried."
Marie calls the dog.
The dog goes into the garden. It isn't on the road.
Peter: "Very good, the dog is in the garden."

The mother comes into the garden. She isn't lying in bed and she isn't sleeping.
Mrs. Schmidt: "Where's the dog?"
Children: "It's here. We're playing with the dog."
Mrs. Schmidt: "Where is your ball?"

Kinder: „Da ist der Ball. Der Hund hat den Ball. Wo ist Vater?"

Frau Schmidt: „Euer Vater liegt im Bett und schläft."

Was ist im Garten? Da ist ein Baum. Ein Vogel ist auf dem Baum.

 **die Sonne**

Ist der Hund auf dem Baum? Nein, der Hund ist nicht auf dem Baum.

die Sonne – **sun**   holen – **get**
scheinen - **shine**   das Tier - **animal**

Was macht die Sonne? Die Sonne scheint.

Was machen die Kinder? Die Kinder spielen.

Was macht die Mutter? Die Mutter geht in den Garten.

Was ist ein Vogel? Der Vogel ist ein Tier.

Der Vogel und der Hund sind Tiere. Es sind zwei Tiere im Garten.

Sind zwei Leute im Garten? Nein, es sind drei Leute im Garten.

Children: "There is the ball. The dog has the ball. Where's father?"

Mrs. Schmidt: "Your father is lying in bed and sleeping."

What is in the garden? There is a tree. A bird is in the tree.

 **ein schöner Garten**

Is the dog on the tree? No, the dog isn't on the tree.

ich hole	wir holen
du holst	ihr holt
er, sie, es holt	sie holen

What is the sun doing? The sun is shining.

What are the children doing? The children are playing.

What's mother doing? Mother is going into the garden.

What is a bird? A bird is an animal.

The bird and the dog are animals. There are two animals in the garden.

Are there two people in the garden? No, there are three people in the garden.

der Vogel

Der Vater kommt. Er geht nicht auf die Straße. Er geht in den Garten.
Herr Schmidt: „Die Sonne scheint, das ist gut. Was macht der Hund?"

der Baum

Peter: „Rex holt den Ball."
Herr Schmidt: „Was macht ihr?"
Kinder: „Wir spielen mit Rex und dem Ball."
Herr Schmidt: „Das ist sehr gut. Spielt ihr auf der Straße?"
Kinder: „Nein, wir spielen nicht auf der Straße. Wir spielen im Garten."

weiß – **white**   schwarz – **black**
blau – **blue**   gelb - **yellow**
grün – **green**   Himmel - **sky**

ich komme	wir kommen
du kommst	ihr kommt
er, sie, es kommt	sie kommen

The father is coming. He isn't going on the road. He's going into the garden.

Mr. Schmidt: "The sun is shining, that's good. What is the dog doing?"

drei Bäume

Peter: "Rex is fetching the ball."

Mr. Schmidt: "What are you (two) doing?"

Children: "We're playing with Rex and the ball."

Mr. Schmidt: "That's very good. Are you playing on the road?"

Children: "No, we aren't playing on the road. We're playing in the garden."

Die Sonne scheint. Sie ist gelb. Ist der Baum gelb? Nein, der Baum ist nicht gelb, er ist grün. Wo ist der Vogel? Der Vogel ist im grünen Baum. Ist der Vogel grün? Nein, der Vogel ist nicht grün. Er ist schwarz. Der schwarze Vogel ist im grünen Baum. Wo ist die gelbe Sonne? Die Sonne ist am Himmel. Ist der Himmel gelb? Nein, der Himmel ist nicht gelb, er ist blau. Und der Hund, ist der Hund schwarz? Nein, er ist nicht schwarz. Der Hund ist weiß.

Ist der Ball weiß? Nein, er ist gelb.

Ist das Bett weiß? Ja, es ist weiß.

Ist der Himmel weiß? Nein, er ist blau.

Ist die Sonne weiß? Nein, sie ist gelb.

Ist der Baum weiß? Nein, er ist grün.

Was ist weiß? Der Hund und das Bett sind weiß.

	Einzahl	**Mehrzahl**
1. Person	ich bin	wir sind
2. Person	du bist	ihr seid
3. Person	er, sie, es ist	sie sind

das Bett

The sun is shining. It's yellow. Is the tree yellow? No, the tree isn't yellow, it's green. Where is the bird? The bird is in the green tree. Is the bird green? No, the bird isn't green. It's black. The black bird is in the green tree.

Where is the yellow sun? The sun is in the sky. Is the sky yellow? No, the sky isn't yellow, it's blue.

And the dog, is the dog black? No, it isn't black. The dog is white.

Is the ball white? No, it's yellow.

Is the bed white? Yes, it's white.

Is the sky white? No, it's blue.

Is the sun white? No, it's yellow.

Is the tree white? No, it's green.

What is white? The dog and the bed are white.

Drittes Kapitel

sagen - **say**

sehen - **see**

die Blume - **flower**

das Haus - **house**

	Einzahl	Mehrzahl
1. Person	ich sehe	wir sehen
2. Person	du siehst	ihr seht
3. Person	er, sie, es sieht	sie sehen

Vater: „Kinder, wo seid ihr?"

Kinder: „Wir sind im Garten."

Vater: „Was seht ihr im Garten?"

Kinder: „Wir sehen einen grünen Baum und einen schwarzen Vogel."

Mutter: „Was siehst du, Marie?"

Marie: „Ich sehe den weißen Hund. Er liegt im Garten. Und was seht ihr?"

Eltern: „Wir sehen die Blumen. Sie sind gelb, blau und weiß."

Was macht der Hund? Er schläft im Garten.

Schlafen die Kinder? Nein, sie schlafen nicht. Sie sagen ihren Eltern was sie im Garten sehen.

ich sage	wir sagen
du sagst	ihr sagt
er, sie, es sagt	sie sagen

Und was sagen die Eltern? Sagen sie den Kindern was sie auf der Straße sehen?

Nein, sie sagen was sie im Garten sehen.

Sind die Kinder auf der Straße?

Third Chapter

 **eine Blume**

Father: "Children, where are you?"
Children: "We're in the garden."
Father: "What do you see in the garden?"
Children: "We see a green tree and a black bird."

Mother: "What do you see, Marie?"
Marie: "I see the white dog. It's lying in the garden. And what do you see?"
Parents: "We see the flowers. They're yellow, blue and white."

What is the dog doing? It's sleeping in the garden.
Are the children sleeping? No, they aren't sleeping. They're telling their parents what they see in the garden.

And what are the parents saying? Are they telling their children what they see on the road?
No, they're saying what they see in the garden.
Are the children on the road?

Nein. Auf der Straße haben die Kinder Angst. Das ist nicht gut. Die Kinder sind im Garten. Das ist gut.

Peter: „Ich habe Angst auf der Straße."

Marie: „Was sagst du? Sagst du, dass du auf dem Baum Angst hast?"

Peter: „Nein, sage ich nicht. Ich sage, dass ich auf der Straße Angst habe."

Peter hat Angst auf der Straße. Er spielt nicht auf der Straße. Er spielt im Garten. Das ist gut.

die Katze - **cat**	schön - **nice**
klein - **little**	stehen - **stand**
groß - **big**	jetzt - **now**

Eine Katze ist auf der Straße. Sie hat Angst und geht in den Garten. Die Kinder sehen die Katze und rufen: „Seht, eine Katze."

Jetzt schläft der Hund nicht. Der weiße Hund sieht die Katze. Jetzt hat die Katze Angst und geht auf den grünen Baum. Ist die Katze groß? Nein, sie ist nicht groß. Sie ist klein. Der Baum ist groß.

Die Eltern stehen im Garten und sagen: „Ja, da ist eine kleine Katze. Die Katze ist auf dem Baum."

Marie: „Das ist eine schöne Katze. Sie ist schwarz."

Peter: „Die Katze hat Angst. Komm her, Rex."

Der Hund geht zu Peter.

Mutter: „Das ist gut."

Jetzt liegt der Hund im Garten. Die kleine Katze sieht den weißen Hund. Sie hat Angst. Das ist nicht gut.

fragen - **ask**	langsam - **slow(ly)**
beide - **both**	laut - **loud**
lachen - **laugh**	zu - **to**

No. The children are afraid on the road. That isn't good. The children are in the garden. That's good.

Peter: "I'm afraid on the road."

Marie: "What are you saying? Are you saying you're afraid on the tree?"

Peter: "No, I'm not saying that. I'm saying that I'm afraid on the road."

Peter is afraid on the road. He doesn't play on the road. He is playing in the garden. That's good.

A cat is on the road. It's afraid and goes into the garden. The children see the cat and call: "Look, a cat."

Now the dog isn't sleeping. The white dog sees the cat. Now the cat is afraid and goes on the green tree. Is the cat big? No, it isn't big. It's small. The tree is big.

The parents are standing in the garden and saying: "Yes, there is a small cat. The cat's in the tree."

Marie: "It's a nice cat. It's black."

Peter: "The cat's afraid. Come here, Rex."

The dog goes to Peter.

Mother: "That's good."

Now the dog is lying in the garden. The little cat sees the white dog. It's afraid. That's not good.

Der Vater geht langsam in das Haus.
„Was machst du?" fragen die Kinder.
„Ich gehe in das Haus," sagt der Vater.

ich habe	wir haben
du hast	ihr habt
er, sie, es hat	sie haben

„Wo ist euer Vater?", fragt die Mutter.
„Vater ist im Haus", sagen die Kinder.
Beide Kinder lachen laut und gehen zum Baum. Die Mutter geht zum Baum.
„Siehst du den Vogel?", fragen die Kinder.
„Ja, ich sehe den Vogel und die Katze", sagt die Mutter.
Der Vogel ist auf der Katze.
Die Mutter lacht und beide Kinder lachen. Da kommt Vater. Er sieht den Vogel und die Katze und lacht. Beide Eltern lachen. Sie lachen sehr laut.
Lacht der Hund? Nein, Rex lacht nicht. Er hat jetzt Angst.
Was macht der Hund? Er geht langsam zu dem Haus.

oben - **up**　　　　　　　　　schnell - **fast**
fliegen - **fly**　　　　　　　springen - **jump**

Die kleine Katze ist oben auf dem Baum. Hat die Katze jetzt Angst? Nein, die kleine Katze hat keine Angst. Die Katze springt in den Garten.
Was macht der Vogel? Der Vogel fliegt schnell.
Was macht die kleine Katze jetzt? Sie geht schnell auf die Straße.

The father slowly walks into the house.
"What are you doing?" the children ask.
"I'm going into the house," father says.

"Where's your father?" mother asks.
"Father's in the house," the children say.
Both children laugh loudly and go to the tree. The mother goes to the tree.
"Do you see the bird?" the children ask.
"Yes, I see the bird and the cat," mother says.
The bird is on the cat.
Mother laughs and both children laugh. Then father comes. He sees the bird and the cat and laughs. Both parents laugh. They are laughing loudly.
Is the dog laughing? No, Rex isn't laughing. He's afraid now. What's the dog doing? He's going to the house

The little cat is up on the tree. Is the cat afraid now? No, the little cat isn't afraid. The cat jumps into the garden.

What's the bird doing? The bird is flying fast.
What is the cat doing now? It's quickly going onto the road.

Was machen die beiden Kinder und ihre Eltern? Sie gehen zu dem schönen Haus.

Der Vater fragt laut: „Ist unser Haus schön?"

„Ja, es ist sehr schön", sagt die Mutter.

Und was sagen die beiden Kinder?

„Unser Haus ist sehr schön. Wir gehen schnell in das schöne Haus."

Was machen die beiden Kinder im Haus? Sie lachen und spielen.

Was macht Rex? Der Hund schläft.

ich schlafe	wir schlafen
du schläfst	ihr schlaft
er, sie, es schläft	sie schlafen

die Katze

What are the two children and their parents doing? They're going to the nice house.

Father asks loudly: "Is our house nice?"

"Yes, it's very nice," mother says.

And what do the two children say?

"Our house is very nice. We're going quickly into the nice house."

What are the two children doing in the house? They are laughing and playing.

What is Rex doing? The dog is sleeping.

das Haus

Viertes Kapitel

das Fenster - **window**	will - **want**
der Boden - **floor**	aus - **out**
sitzen - **sit**	das Auto - **car**

Peter sitzt auf dem Boden und spielt mit einem Auto. Das Auto ist schön und blau.
Marie steht am Fenster. Sie sieht aus dem Fenster auf die Straße. Auf der Straße sieht sie Autos.
Was sieht sie im Garten? Im Garten sieht sie Blumen und Bäume. Was sieht sie auf den Bäumen? Sie sieht Vögel auf den Bäumen.
„Was machst du, Peter?", fragt Marie.
„Ich sitze auf dem Boden und spiele mit meinen Autos", sagt Peter. „Ich habe vier Autos. Da ist ein blaues Auto, ein gelbes Auto, ein schwarzes Auto und ein weißes Auto. Meine Autos sind sehr schön. Und was machst du?"
Marie lacht. „Ich stehe am Fenster. Ich sehe neun Autos, sieben Bäume und acht Blumen. Da sind vier gelbe Blumen, drei weiße Blumen und eine blaue Blume."
„Komm schnell und spiel mit mir", sagt Peter.
„Nein", sagt Marie, „ich will nicht mit Autos spielen."

das Brot - **bread**	essen - **eat**
das Wasser - **water**	trinken - **drink**
mir – (with) **me**	nehmen - **take**

„Marie, spiel mit mir", sagt Peter laut.
„Nein, ich will nicht mit deinen Autos spielen. Ich will essen und trinken."
„Was willst du essen und trinken?", fragt Peter.
„Ich will Brot essen und Wasser trinken", sagt Marie.
Marie geht in die Küche und nimmt ein Brot.

Fourth Chapter

ich will	wir wollen
du willst	ihr wollt
er, sie, es will	sie wollen

Peter is sitting on the floor and playing with a car. The car is nice and blue.

Marie is standing at the window. She's looking out of the window at the road. On the road she sees cars.

What does she see in the garden? In the garden she sees flowers and trees. What does she see in the trees? She sees birds in the trees.

"What are you doing, Peter?" Marie asks.

"I'm sitting on the floor and playing with my cars," Peter says. "I have four cars. There is a blue car, a yellow car, a black car and a white car. My cars are very nice. And what are you doing?"

Marie laughs. "I'm standing at the window. I see nine cars, seven trees and eight flowers. There are four yellow flowers, three white flowers and one blue flower."

"Come quickly and play with me," Peter says.

"No," Marie says, "I don't want to play with cars.

ich nehme	wir nehmen
du nimmst	ihr nehmt
er, sie, es nimmt	sie nehmen

"Marie, play with me," Peter says loudly.

"No, I don't want to play with your cars. I want to eat and drink."

"What do you want to eat and drink?" Peter asks.

"I want to eat bread and drink water," Marie says.

Marie goes into the kitchen and takes some bread.

die Küche - **kitchen**

Sie nimmt Wasser. Sie trinkt das Wasser und isst das Brot.
Marie ruft laut: „Peter, ich esse Brot und trinke Wasser. Willst
du essen und trinken?"
Peter kommt in die Küche.
„Ja", sagt er, „ich will Brot essen und Wasser trinken."
Jetzt sitzt Peter nicht auf dem Boden. Er steht in der Küche
und isst Brot und trinkt Wasser.

ich esse	wir essen
du isst	ihr esst
er, sie, es isst	sie essen

der Tag - **day**   weil - **because**
die Stadt - **town**   hören - **hear**
kaufen - **buy**   gern - **gladly**

Beide Kinder essen und trinken in der Küche. Und was
machen ihre Eltern? Sind die Eltern in der Küche und essen
und trinken?
Die Mutter ist nicht in der Küche. Sie ist in der Stadt, weil sie
Brot kaufen will. Sie kauft gerne Brot in der Stadt.
Der Vater ist im Garten, weil es ein schöner Tag ist. Er ist
gerne im Garten. Die Sonne scheint und er hört die Vögel.
Hört die Mutter Vögel in der Stadt? Nein, sie hört Autos in
der Stadt.
Hört der Vater Autos im Garten? Nein, er hört Vögel im
Garten.

ich höre	wir hören
du hörst	ihr hört
er, sie, es hört	sie hören

She takes some water. She drinks the water and eats the bread.
Marie calls loudly: "Peter, I'm eating bread and drinking
water. Do you want to eat and drink?"
Peter comes into the kitchen.
"Yes," he says, "I want to eat bread and drink water."
Now Peter isn't sitting on the floor. He's standing in the
kitchen and eating bread and drinking water.

die Küche

Both children are eating and drinking in the kitchen. And
what are their parents doing? Are their parents in the kitchen
and eating and drinking?
Mother isn't in the kitchen. She's in town because she wants
to buy bread. She likes buying bread in town.
Father is in the garden because it's a nice day. He likes being
in the garden. The sun is shining and he hears the birds.
Does mother hear birds in town? No, she hears cars in town.

Does father hear cars in the garden? No, he hears birds in the
garden.

heute - **today**   der Schuh - **shoe**
das Eis - **ice cream**   neu - **new**
dann - **then**   rot - **red**

Heute ist Frau Schmidt in der Stadt. Sie geht gerne in die Stadt, weil sie gerne einkauft.

ich gehe einkaufen	I go shopping

Was kauft Frau Schmidt heute? Sie kauft Brot, weil ihre Kinder gerne Brot essen. Dann kauft sie ein Eis, weil sie gerne Eis isst. Die Schuhe von Frau Schmidt sind nicht schön, weil sie alt sind. Frau Schmidt will neue Schuhe kaufen. Sie kauft Schuhe sehr gerne. Jetzt kauft sie neue Schuhe. Sind die neuen Schuhe rot? Nein, die neuen Schuhe von Frau Schmidt sind schwarz. Sie kauft schwarze Schuhe. Jetzt lacht Frau Schmidt, weil sie die Schuhe sehr gerne hat.

ich habe die Schuhe gerne	I like the shoes

Frau Schmidt ist sehr gerne in der Stadt, weil sie ein Eis isst und schöne neue Schuhe kauft.
Herr Schmidt ist gerne im Garten, weil er die Sonne sieht und die Vögel hört.
Die Kinder sind gerne in der Küche, weil sie gerne Brot essen und Wasser trinken.
Was macht Rex gerne? Der Hund spielt gerne mit dem Ball.

zwei Schuhe

Today Mrs. Schmidt is in town. She likes going into town because she likes going shopping.

What is Mrs. Schmidt buying today? She is buying bread because her children like eating bread. Then she buys an ice cream because she likes eating ice cream. Mrs. Schmidt's shoes are not nice because they are old. Mrs. Schmidt wants to buy new shoes. She likes buying shoes very much. Now she's buying new shoes. Are the new shoes red? No, Mrs. Schmidt's new shoes are black. She's buying black shoes. Now Mrs. Schmidt is laughing because she likes the shoes very much.

ein Eis

Mrs. Schmidt is very happy to be in town because she's eating ice cream and buying nice new shoes.
Mr. Schmidt is happy to be in the garden because he sees the sun and hears the birds.
The children are happy to be in the kitchen because they like eating bread and drinking water.
What does Rex like to do? The dog likes playing with the ball.

sprechen - **speak**	viel – **much, many**
mehr - **more**	denken - **think**
tragen - **carry**	stellen/legen – **put** (on), **lie**

Frau Schmidt geht jetzt nach Hause. Sie trägt ihre neuen Schuhe in einer Tasche. Sie denkt an die Schuhe und sie will mehr Schuhe kaufen. Sie kauft gerne viele neue Schuhe.

ich gehe nach Hause	**I am going home**

Hat Frau Schmidt alte Schuhe gerne? Nein, sie hat neue Schuhe gerne.
Jetzt ist Frau Schmidt in ihrem Haus. Sie stellt die neuen Schuhe auf den Boden. Sie geht mit dem Brot in die Küche.
Die Kinder sehen das Brot. Sie sind glücklich.
Herr Schmidt sieht die neuen schwarzen Schuhe. Er ist nicht glücklich. Er spricht mit Frau Schmidt.
„Du hast sehr viele Schuhe."
Jetzt ist Frau Schmidt nicht glücklich.
„Meine Schuhe sind alt. Ich will schöne neue Schuhe. Neue Schuhe sind gut, alte Schuhe sind nicht gut."
Marie: „Ich will mehr Brot essen."
Die Mutter sieht das neue Brot nicht mehr. Die beiden Kinder haben das Brot gegessen.

haben gegessen	**have eaten**

„Ich esse Brot gerne", sagt Peter und lacht.
Frau Schmidt lacht nicht. Sie ist nicht mehr glücklich. Sie nimmt die neuen Schuhe und trägt sie aus der Küche.
Lachen die Kinder jetzt? Nein, sie lachen nicht mehr.
Ist Herr Schmidt glücklich? Nein, er ist nicht glücklich.

glücklich - **happy**

Mrs. Schmidt is going home now. She's carrying her new shoes in a bag. She's thinking about her shoes and she wants to buy more shoes. She likes buying lots of new shoes.

Does Mrs. Schmidt like old shoes? No, she likes new shoes.

Now Mrs. Schmidt is in her house. She puts the new shoes on the floor. She goes into the kitchen with the bread.
The children see the bread. They are happy.
Mr. Schmidt sees the new black shoes. He isn't happy. He talks with Mrs. Schmidt.
"You have so many shoes."
Now Mrs. Schmidt isn't happy.
"My shoes are old. I want nice new shoes. New shoes are good, old shoes are not good."
Marie: "I want to eat more bread."
Mother doesn't see the new bread anymore. The two children have eaten the bread.

"I like eating bread," Peter says and laughs.
Frau Schmidt isn't laughing. She isn't happy anymore. She takes her new shoes and carries them out of the kitchen.
Are the children laughing now? No, they aren't laughing anymore. Is Mr. Schmidt happy? No, he isn't happy.

Fünftes Kapitel

war - **was**
waren - **were**
immer - **always**
wieder - **again**

das Geld - **money**
geben - **give**
der Tisch – **table**
der Abend - **evening**

Heute Abend spricht die Mutter mit Marie.
Marie: „Was hast du heute gemacht?"
Mutter: „Ich bin heute in die Stadt gegangen."
Marie: „Das ist schön."
Mutter: „Ja, ich habe eingekauft."
Marie: „Was hast du gekauft?"
Mutter: „Ich habe Brot gekauft. Dann habe ich ein Eis gekauft. Ich habe das Eis gegessen. Dann habe ich neue Schuhe gekauft."

das Geld

Frau Schmidt geht immer gerne in die Stadt. Sie kauft immer gerne ein. Heute ist sie in die Stadt gegangen. Sie hat Brot, ein Eis und neue Schuhe gekauft. Sie hat das Brot und die Schuhe nach Hause getragen. Hat sie das Eis nach Hause getragen? Nein, sie hat es in der Stadt gegessen. Frau Schmidt war heute sehr glücklich.

Fifth Chapter

ich war	wir waren
du warst	ihr wart
er, sie, es war	sie waren

This evening mother is talking with Marie.
Marie: "What did you do today?"
Mother: "Today I went into town."
Marie: "That's nice."
Mother: "Yes, I went shopping."
Marie: "What did you buy?"
Mother: "I bought bread. Then I bought an ice cream. I ate the ice cream. Then I bought new shoes.

die Münzen - coins

Mrs. Schmidt always likes going into town. She always likes going shopping. Today she went into town. She bought bread, an ice cream and new shoes. She carried the bread and the shoes home. Did she carry the ice cream home?
No, she ate it in town. Mrs. Schmidt was very happy today.

Waren die Kinder heute glücklich? Ja, sie waren glücklich. Was haben sie gemacht?

Peter hat mit seinen Autos gespielt. Marie hat Bäume, Blumen und Autos aus dem Fenster gesehen.

Dann sind die Kinder in die Küche gegangen. Sie haben Brot gegessen und Wasser getrunken.

Und was hat Herr Schmidt gemacht?

Er war im Garten. Er hat die Sonne gesehen und die Vögel gehört. Er war gerne im Garten. Er war sehr glücklich im Garten. Geht Herr Schmidt immer in den Garten? Nein, nicht immer.

das Brot

Was hat Frau Schmidt am Abend gemacht?

Sie ist nach Hause gegangen. Sie hat die Schuhe auf den Boden gestellt und sie hat das Brot auf den Tisch gelegt. Sie hat ihren Kindern Brot gegeben. Die beiden Kinder waren sehr glücklich. Sie hat an ihre neuen Schuhe gedacht und war glücklich. Dann hat sie mit ihrem Mann gesprochen.

Herr Schmidt hat die neuen Schuhe gesehen. Er hat nicht an die neuen Schuhe gedacht. Er hat an das Geld gedacht. Er war nicht glücklich.

Hat Frau Schmidt an das Geld gedacht? Nein, sie hat an ihre neuen Schuhe gedacht.

Haben die Kinder an das Geld gedacht? Nein, sie haben an das Brot gedacht. Sie haben das Brot gegessen.

Were the children happy today? Yes, they were happy.
What did they do?
Peter played with his cars. Marie saw trees, flowers and cars from the window.
Then the children went into the kitchen. They ate bread and drank water.
And what did Mr. Schmidt do?
He was in the garden. He saw the sun and heard the birds. He liked being in the garden. He was very happy in the garden.
Does Mr. Schmidt always go into the garden? No, not always.

 ein Stück Brot

What did Mrs. Schmidt do in the evening?
She went home. She put the shoes on the floor and she put the bread on the table. She gave her children some bread.
The two children were very happy. She thought about her new shoes and was very happy.
Then she talked with her husband.
Mr. Schmidt saw the new shoes. He didn't think about the new shoes. He thought about the money. He wasn't happy.

Did Mrs. Schmidt think about the money? No, she thought abought her new shoes.
Did the children think about money? No, they were thinking about the bread. They ate the bread.

Haben die Eltern Brot gegessen? Nein, sie haben das Brot nicht gegessen und sie haben das Wasser nicht getrunken. Die Mutter hat an ihre neuen Schuhe gedacht und der Vater hat an das Geld gedacht.

brauchen - **need**	Stück - **piece**
bekommen - **get**	noch - **still; another**
für - **for**	alle - **all**

Was will Frau Schmidt? Sie braucht neue Schuhe. Sie will neue Schuhe kaufen. Heute ist sie einkaufen gegangen und sie hat neue Schuhe gekauft.

Was will Herr Schmidt? Er will im Garten sein. Heute war er im Garten. Er hat die Blumen und Bäume gesehen und er hat die Vögel gehört.

Was wollen die Kinder? Die Kinder wollen spielen, essen und trinken. Heute haben sie gespielt, gegessen und getrunken.

Und was will Rex? Der Hund will mit dem Ball spielen und schlafen. Heute hat er gespielt und geschlafen. Hat er im Bett geschlafen? Nein, er ist nicht im Bett gelegen, er hat auf dem Boden geschlafen.

Was hat die Mutter heute Abend gesagt?

„Ich habe Brot für euch."

Was hat sie die Kinder gefragt?

„Wollt ihr ein Stück Brot haben?"

Was haben die Kinder gesagt?

„Ja, wir wollen Brot essen. Gib uns bitte das Brot."

bitte - **please**

Gibt die Mutter ihnen Brot? Ja, sie gibt Marie ein Stück Brot und Peter ein Stück Brot. Sie hat den Kindern Brot gegeben.

Did the parents eat any bread? No, they didn't eat bread and they didn't drink any water. Mother thought about her new shoes and father thought about the money.

ich brauche	wir brauchen
du brauchst	ihr braucht
er, sie, es braucht	sie brauchen

What does Mrs. Schmidt want? She needs new shoes. She wants to buy new shoes. Today she went shopping and she bought new shoes.

What does Mr. Schmidt want? He wants to be in the garden. Today he was in the garden. He saw the flowers and the trees and he heard the birds.

What do the children want? The children want to play, eat and drink. Today they played, ate and drank.

And what does Rex want? The dog wants to play with the ball and sleep. Today he played and slept. Did he sleep in bed? No, he didn't lie in bed, he slept on the floor.

What did mother say this evening?
"I have bread for you."
What did she ask the children?
"Do you want to have a piece of bread?"
What did the children say?
"Yes, we want to eat bread. Please give us the bread."

Does the mother give them any bread? Yes, she gives Marie a piece of bread and Peter a piece of bread. She gave the children some bread.

ich gebe	wir geben
du gibst	ihr gebt
er, sie, es gibt	sie geben

Peter hat das Stück Brot gegessen. Was hat er dann gesagt?
„Gib mir bitte noch ein Stück Brot."
Seine Mutter hat ihm noch ein Stück Brot gegeben.

Was haben sie heute alle gemacht?

Rex hat mit dem Ball gespielt. Er ist in das Haus gegangen und er hat geschlafen.
Der Vater hat Bäume gesehen und er hat Vögel gehört. Er hat mit seiner Frau gesprochen.
Die Mutter ist einkaufen gegangen. Sie hat Brot und Schuhe gekauft. Sie hat ihren Kindern Brot gegeben.
Die Kinder haben mit dem Hund gespielt. Sie haben von ihrer Mutter Brot bekommen. Sie haben Brot gegessen und sie haben Wasser getrunken.
Wo sind sie jetzt alle? Sie sind alle in ihrem Haus. Sie sind zuhause.

ich bin zuhause	**I am at home**

Wo waren sie?
Frau Schmidt war in der Stadt.
Herr Schmidt war im Garten.
Die beiden Kinder und der Hund waren im Haus.

An was haben sie alle gedacht?
Frau Schmidt hat an ihre neuen Schuhe gedacht.
Herr Schmidt hat an sein Geld gedacht.
Die Kinder haben an das Brot gedacht.

ich bekomme	wir bekommen
du bekommst	ihr bekommt
er, sie, es bekommt	sie bekommen

Peter ate the piece of bread. What did he say then?
"Please give me another piece of bread."
His mother gave him another piece of bread.

What did they all do today?

Rex played with the ball. He went into the house and slept.

Father saw trees and heard birds. He talked with his wife.

Mother went shopping. She bought bread and shoes. She gave her children some bread.
The children played with the dog. They got bread from their mother. They ate the bread and drank some water.

Where are they all now? They are all in their house. They are at home.

ich gehe nach Hause	**I am going home**

Where were they?
Mrs. Schmidt was in town.
Mr. Schmidt was in the garden.
The two children and the dog were in the house.

What were they all thinking about?
Mrs. Schmidt was thinking about her new shoes.
Mr. Schmidt was thinking about his money.
The children were thinking about the bread.

Der Hund hat an den Ball gedacht.

als - **when**

Der Bruder und die Schwester waren heute sehr glücklich. Die Mutter war glücklich in der Stadt, weil sie eingekauft hat. Der Vater war glücklich im Garten. Er war nicht glücklich als er die neuen Schuhe seiner Frau gesehen hat. Seine Frau war nicht glücklich als sie mit ihm am Abend gesprochen hat.

 **eine große Stadt**

 **eine kleine Stadt**

The dog was thinking about the ball.

The brother and the sister were very happy today.
Mother was happy in town because she went shopping.
Father was happy in the garden. He wasn't happy when he
saw his wife's new shoes. His wife wasn't happy when she
talked with him in the evening.

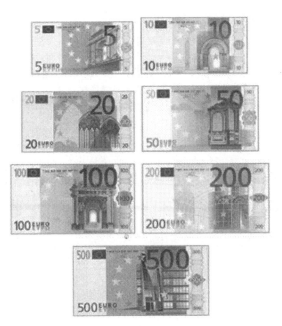

Euro Banknoten – euro bills/banknotes

Sechstes Kapitel

die Schule - **school**   die Tür - **door**
fahren - **drive**   der Weg - **way, path**
der Fuß - **foot**   tun/machen - **do**

Was macht die Familie Schmidt heute?
Der Vater fährt mit seinem Auto in die Stadt.
Der Bruder und die Schwester gehen in die Schule. Sie fahren nicht mit dem Auto, sie gehen zu Fuß.
Die Mutter ist mit dem Hund zu Hause.
Herr Schmidt macht die Tür auf und geht aus dem Haus. Dann macht er die Tür zu. Er geht zu seinem roten Auto. Als er sein rotes Auto sieht lacht er und ist glücklich.
Er sagt „Hier ist mein schönes rotes Auto. Ich habe mein Auto gerne." Dann fährt er in die Stadt. Was sieht er auf dem Weg in die Stadt? Er sieht sehr viele Autos auf der Straße. Viele Leute fahren mit dem Auto in die Stadt. Jetzt fährt er nicht mehr schnell, er fährt sehr langsam. Als er langsam fährt, ist Herr Schmidt nicht mehr glücklich.

Es sind sehr viele Autos auf der Straße.

Dann machen die beiden Kinder die Tür auf und gehen aus dem Haus. Sie gehen jetzt in die Schule. Was sehen sie auf dem Weg in die Schule? Sehen sie viele Autos?

Sixth Chapter

eine Tür	zwei Türen
ein Weg	zwei Wege
ein Fuß	zwei Füße

What is the Schmidt family doing today?
Father is driving into town with his car.
The brother and sister are going to school. They aren't driving
a car, they're going on foot.
Mother is at home with the dog.
Mr. Schmidt opens the door and leaves the house.
Then he closes the door. He goes to his red car. When he sees
his red car he laughs and is happy.
He says: "Here is my nice red car. I like my car."
Then he drives into town. What does he see on the way into
town? He sees a great many cars on the road. Many people are
driving into town with their cars. Now he isn't driving fast
anymore, he's driving slowly. When he's driving slowly Mr.
Schmidt isn't happy anymore.

ein Stau – a traffic jam

Then the two children open the door and leave the house.
They're going to school now. What do they see on the way to
school? Do they see many cars?

53

Nein, sie fahren nicht mit dem Auto in die Schule. Sie gehen zu Fuß in die Schule. Auf dem Weg in die Schule sehen sie viele grüne Bäume und sie hören Vögel in den Bäumen. Viele Vögel fliegen von Baum zu Baum. Die Kinder fliegen nicht, sie gehen zu Fuß. Peter und Marie gehen immer zu Fuß in die Schule. Nicht alle Kinder gehen zu Fuß in die Schule. Viele Kinder fahren mit dem Auto in die Schule.

Die Mutter ist zu Hause. Sie geht mit Rex in den Garten und lacht. Die Sonne scheint, der Garten ist schön und sie hat nichts zu tun.

ich fahre	wir fahren
du fährst	ihr fahrt
er, sie, es fährt	sie fahren

die Klasse - **class**   die Stunde - **hour**
allein - **alone**   arbeiten - **work**
lesen - **read**   das Buch - **book**

Jetzt sind alle Kinder in der Schule. Sind Peter und Marie in einer Klasse? Nein, sie sind in zwei Klassen. Die Kinder in Peters Klasse lesen ein Buch. Es ist ein sehr gutes Buch und die Kinder lesen es gerne.
In Maries Klasse arbeiten die Kinder. Sie arbeiten nicht gerne. Sie wollen spielen und Bücher lesen.
Die Kinder sind fünf Stunden in der Schule. Dann gehen sie nach Hause. Auf dem Weg nach Hause spricht Marie mit Peter.
„Ich habe heute viel gearbeitet", sagt Marie.
„Ich habe ein Buch gelesen", sagt Peter. „Liest du gerne Bücher?"
„Ja, ich lese gerne Bücher. Ich will in deiner Klasse sein", sagt Marie.

No, they aren't driving to school in a car. They're going to school on foot. On the way to school they see many green trees and they hear birds in the trees. Many birds are flying from tree to tree. The children aren't flying, they're going on foot. Peter and Marie always go to school on foot. Many children go to school by car.

Mother is at home. She goes into the garden with Rex and laughs. The sun is shining, the garden is nice and there's nothing she has to do.

ich arbeite	wir arbeiten
du arbeitest	ihr arbeitet
er, sie, es arbeitet	sie arbeiten

Now all the children are at school. Are Peter and Marie in one class? No, they are in two classes. The children in Peter's class are reading a book. It's a very good book and the children like reading it.
In Marie's class the children are doing work. They don't like working. They want to play and read books.
The children are at school for five hours. Then they go home. On the way home Marie is talking with Peter.

"I did a lot of work today," Marie says.
"I read a book," Peter says. "Do you like reading books?"

"Yes, I like reading books. I want to be in your class," Marie says.

„Wir haben Bücher gelesen und ihr habt fünf Stunden gearbeitet", sagt Peter und lacht. Er ist sehr glücklich.
Marie ist jetzt nicht mehr glücklich. Sie ist unglücklich.

unglücklich - **unhappy**

Herr Schmidt hat in der Stadt gearbeitet. Er hat acht Stunden gearbeitet. Dann ist er mit dem Auto nach Hause gefahren. Er ist in das Haus gegangen und hat mit seiner Frau gesprochen.
„Heute habe ich acht Stunden gearbeitet", sagt Herr Schmidt. „Dann bin ich nach Hause gefahren. Ich habe eine Stunde gebraucht nach Hause zu fahren. Was hast du heute getan?"
Frau Schmidt lacht. „Ich war heute allein zu Hause. Ich war im Garten. Ich bin in der Sonne gelegen und ich habe geschlafen."

auch - **also**

„Rex war auch im Garten. Er hat auch geschlafen", sagt Frau Schmidt.
Jetzt ist Herr Schmidt unglücklich. Er lacht nicht. Er ist heute nicht im Garten gelegen und er hat nicht geschlafen.
„Ich will auch im Garten liegen und schlafen", sagt Herr Schmidt zu seiner Frau.

muss – **must, have to**	kann - **can**
erzählen - **tell about**	richtig - **right**
bleiben - **stay**	schreiben - **write**

Marie erzählt ihren Eltern von der Schule.
„Heute habe ich viel gearbeitet. Ich habe geschrieben und gelesen."
„Kannst du richtig schreiben?", fragt der Vater.

"We were reading books and you worked for five hours," Peter says and laughs. He is very happy.
Marie isn't happy anymore. She is unhappy.

Mr. Schmidt worked in town. He worked for eight hours.
Then he went home by car. He went into the house and he talked with his wife.
"Today I worked for eight hours," Mr. Schmidt says.
"Then I drove home. It took me one hour to drive home. What did you do today?"
Mrs. Schmidt laughs. "I was home alone today. I was in the garden. I lay in the sun and I slept."

"Rex was in the garden too. He also slept," Mrs. Schmidt says.
Now Mr. Schmidt is unhappy. He isn't laughing. He didn't lie in the garden today and he didn't sleep.
"I also want to lie in the garden and sleep," Mr. Schmidt says to his wife.

Marie tells her parents about school.
"Today I did a lot of work. I wrote and I read."

"Can you write correctly?" father asks.

„Ja, ich kann richtig schreiben. Ich habe alles richtig geschrieben."

„Und du, Peter", sagt die Mutter, „hast du viel gearbeitet? Hast du alles richtig geschrieben?"

„Ich habe heute nichts geschrieben. Ich habe heute in der Schule ein Buch gelesen."

„Das ist nicht gut", sagt der Vater. „Das ist sehr schlecht."

schlecht - **bad**

„Du musst in der Schule arbeiten und du musst richtig schreiben. Wir müssen alle richtig schreiben können. Du hast in der Schule nichts geschrieben, dann musst du jetzt schreiben."

Jetzt ist Peter unglücklich.

„Ich will nicht schreiben", sagt er. „Ich will jetzt spielen."

ich muss	wir müssen
du musst	ihr müsst
er, sie, es muss	sie müssen

Jetzt sitzt Peter am Tisch und schreibt. Kann er gut schreiben? Nein, er schreibt sehr schlecht. Seine Eltern sind unglücklich. Ist seine Schwester unglücklich? Nein, sie spielt und ist glücklich.

Die Mutter liest was Peter schreibt. „Du kannst nicht richtig schreiben", sagt die Mutter zu Peter. „Du schreibst sehr schlecht, also musst du mehr schreiben. Du musst richtig schreiben können."

Peter will nicht schreiben. Er will seiner Mutter von der Schule erzählen. Seine Mutter will es nicht hören. Sie hat gelesen was er geschrieben hat und sie hat gesehen, dass es sehr schlecht ist.

"Yes, I can write correctly. I wrote everything correctly."

"And you, Peter," mother says, "did you do a lot of work?
Did you write everything correctly?"
"I didn't write anything today. I read a book at school today."

"That isn't good," father says. "That's very bad."

Er schreibt schlecht.	**He writes badly.**

"You have to work at school and you have to write correctly.
We all have to be able to write correctly. You didn't write
anything at school, so you have to write now."

Now Peter is unhappy.
"I don't want to write," he says. "I want to play now."

Now Peter is sitting at the table and he's writing. Can he write
well? No, he writes very badly. His parents are unhappy.
Is his sister unhappy? No, she's playing and she's happy.

His mother is reading what Peter is writing. "You can't write
correctly," mother says to Peter. "You write very badly, so
you have to write more. You have to be able to write
correctly."
Peter doesn't want to write. He wants to tell his mother about
school. His mother doesn't want to hear about it. She has read
what he has written and she has seen that it's very bad.

dass - that

Die Mutter hat gesehen, dass Peter sehr schlecht schreibt. Sie will nicht, dass er von der Schule erzählt. Sie will, dass er mehr schreibt. Sie will, dass er richtig schreiben kann.
Kann Peter gut lesen? Ja, er hat viel in der Schule gelesen. Will seine Mutter, dass er mehr liest? Nein, sie will, dass er mehr arbeitet.

Was hat Herr Schmidt erzählt? Er hat erzählt, dass er acht Stunden gearbeitet hat und dass er eine Stunde im Auto nach Hause gefahren ist.
Frau Schmidt hat erzählt, dass sie alleine zu Hause war und dass sie im Garten geschlafen hat.
Marie hat erzählt, dass sie fünf Stunden in der Schule gearbeitet hat und dass sie viel geschrieben hat.
Peter erzählt, dass er in der Klasse ein Buch gelesen hat.

Die Kinder gehen zu Fuß in die Schule

Mother has seen that Peter writes very badly. She doesn't want that he tells about school. She wants him to write more. She wants him to be able to write correctly.

Can Peter read well? Yes, he read a lot at school.

Does his mother want him to read more? No, she wants him to do more work.

What did Mr. Schmidt tell about? He said that he worked for eight hours and that it took him one hour to drive home.

Mrs. Schmidt says that she was alone at home and that she slept in the garden.

Marie says that she worked for five hours at school and that she wrote a lot.

Peter says that he read a book in class.

Siebtes Kapitel

die Woche - **week**
singen - **sing**
setzen - **sit**
sich - **herself, himself**

die Hand - **hand**
der Wald - **forest**
der Stein - **stone**
rennen - **run**

Was wird die Familie Schmidt in einer Woche tun?
In einer Woche werden sie in den Wald gehen. Werden sie zu
Fuß gehen? Nein, sie werden mit dem Auto fahren. Herr
Schmidt wird das Auto fahren. Die Familie Schmidt geht
gerne in den Wald. Im Wald werden die Eltern Hand in Hand
gehen. Marie wird sich auf einen großen Stein setzen und
singen. Sie singt gerne im Wald. Peter will sich nicht auf
einen Stein setzen und er will nicht singen. Er wird im Wald
rennen, weil er gerne rennt.

 **der Wald**

Was werden sie im Wald sehen? Sie werden viele Bäume und
Tiere sehen. Was für Tiere gibt es im Wald? Es gibt viele
Vögel im Wald. Die Leute werden die Vögel im Wald hören.
Werden sie die Vögel in den Bäumen sehen? Nein, die Vögel
sind oben auf den Bäumen. Da können die Leute sie nicht
sehen.

nach - **after**

Seventh Chapter

What is the Schmidt family going to do in a week?
In one week they're going to go in the forest. Are they going to go on foot? No, they're going to go by car. Mr. Schmidt is going to drive the car. The Schmidt family like going into the forest. In the forest the parents will be walking hand in hand. Marie will sit on a large stone and sing. She likes to sing in the forest. Peter doesn't want to sit on a rock and he doesn't want to sing. He is going to run in the forest because he likes running.

 **der Stein**

What are they going to see in the forest? They are going to see many trees and animals. What animals are there in the forest? There are many birds in the forest. The people will hear the birds in the forest.
Will they see the birds in the trees? No, the birds are up in the trees. People can't see them there.

die Uhr - **a watch**   die Maus - **mouse**
die Zeit - **time**   das Auge - **eye**
dürfen - **be allowed to**   fangen - **catch**

Eine Woche später liegt die Familie Schmidt in ihren Betten und schläft. Die Sonne geht auf. Die Familie steht auf und geht in die Küche. Die Mutter stellt Essen und Trinken auf den Tisch. Sie sehen aus dem Fenster. Es ist eine schöner Tag. Die Sonne scheint und der Himmel ist blau.
Nach dem Essen sieht der Vater auf seine Uhr.
„Es ist Zeit, dass wir gehen", sagt er.

 **die Uhr**

Peter macht die Tür auf und die Familie geht zum Auto. Herr Schmidt fährt schnell, weil er gerne im Wald ist. Fährt er mit dem Auto in den Wald? Nein, er stellt das Auto vor dem Wald ab. Dann geht die Familie zu Fuß in den Wald.
„Dürfen wir im Wald rennen?", fragt Peter.
„Ja, das dürft ihr", sagt die Mutter.
Peter ist glücklich und sagt: „Komm Marie, renn mit mir."
„Ich will nicht rennen", sagt Marie. „Ich will langsam gehen."
Also rennt Peter alleine.
Die Eltern gehen Hand in Hand im Wald. Sie gehen gerne im Wald und sprechen miteinander.

miteinander - **with one another**

64

A week later the Schmidt family are lying in their beds sleeping. The sun rises. The family get up and go into the kitchen. The mother puts food and drinks on the table.
They look out of the window. It's a nice day.
The sun is shining and the sky is blue.
After the meal father looks at his watch.
"It's time to go," he says.

ich darf	wir dürfen
du darfst	ihr dürft
er, sie, es darf	sie dürfen

Peter opens the door and the family go to the car. Mr. Schmidt drives fast because he likes to be in the forest. Does he drive into the forest with his car? No, he parks the car in front of the forest. Then the family go into the forest on foot.
"Are we allowed to run in the forest?" Peter asks.
"Yes, you may," mother says.
Peter is happy and says "Come Marie, run with me."
"I don't want to run," Marie says. "I want to walk slowly."
So Peter runs on his own.
The parents are walking hand in hand in the forest. They like walking in the forest and they are talking with one another.

Sprechen der Bruder und die Schwester miteinander?
Nein, Peter rennt alleine im Wald und Marie geht langsam.
Dann sieht Marie einen sehr großen Stein. Sie setzt sich auf
den Stein und singt. Sie ist jetzt sehr glücklich. Nach einiger
Zeit sieht Marie eine kleine schwarze Maus.

nach einiger Zeit - after some time

 **die kleine schwarze Maus**

Dann kommt eine große weiße Katze. Die Katze will die
Maus fangen. Die Maus rennt und die Katze rennt schnell.
Wird die Katze die Maus fangen? Ja, die Katze fängt die
Maus. Marie macht große Augen.
Jetzt hört Marie ihre Mutter rufen: „Marie, wo bist du?"
Marie steht auf und geht schnell zu ihrer Mutter.
„Was hast du gemacht?", fragt die Mutter.
„Ich bin auf einem sehr großen Stein gesessen und ich habe
gesungen. Dann habe ich eine kleine schwarze Maus gesehen.
Eine große weiße Katze ist gekommen und hat die Maus
gefangen."
Dann weint Marie.

weinen - cry
warum - why

Peter kommt und sieht seine Schwester weinen.
„Warum weinst du?", fragt er.
Marie erzählt ihm von der Katze und der Maus.

Are the brother and sister talking with one another?
No, Peter is running alone through the forest and Marie is walking slowly. Then Marie sees a very big stone. She sits down on the stone and sings. Now she's very happy. After some time Marie sees a little mouse.

zwei Mäuse

Then a big white cat comes. The cat wants to catch the mouse. The mouse runs and the cat runs fast.
Will the cat catch the mouse? Yes, the cat catches the mouse.
Marie's eyes open wide.
Then Marie hears her mother calling "Marie, where are you?"
Marie stands up and quickly goes to her mother.
"What have you been doing?" the mother asks.
"I was sitting on a very big stone and I was singing. Then I saw a little black mouse.
A big white cat came and caught the mouse."

Then Marie cries.

Peter comes and sees his sister crying.
"Why are you crying?" he asks.
Marie tells him about the cat and the mouse.

„Weine nicht, Marie", sagt ihr Bruder. „Katzen fangen immer Mäuse. Katzen müssen auch essen."
Jetzt weint Marie nicht mehr.

ich fange	wir fangen
du fängst	ihr fangt
er, sie, es fängt	sie fangen

werfen - **throw**

„Und was hast du gemacht, Peter?", fragt sein Vater.
„Ich bin im Wald gerannt", erzählt Peter. „Ich habe viele Steine ins Wasser geworfen."
„Warum hast du die Steine ins Wasser geworfen?", fragt seine Mutter.
„Ich habe die Steine ins Wasser geworfen, weil ich es gerne mache."
Seine Eltern lachen, weil sie glücklich sind, dass er glücklich ist.

das Pferd - **horse**   dick - **thick, fat**
finden - **find**   hoch - **high**
das Ei - **egg**   fallen - **fall**

Dann hören sie ein Tier. Es ist ein großes Tier. Was ist es für ein Tier? Es ist ein Pferd. Das Pferd geht langsam durch den Wald.

durch - **through**

Es ist ein schönes Pferd. Hoch oben auf dem Pferd sitzt eine dicke Frau. Sie ist glücklich im Wald.

"Don't cry, Marie," her brother says. "Cats always catch mice. Cats also have to eat."
Now Marie isn't crying anymore.

das Pferd ist schnell

"And what did you do, Peter?" his father asks.
"I was running in the forest," Peter says, "I threw many stones into the water."
"Why did you throw the stones into the water?" his mother asks.
"I threw the stones into the water because I like doing it."

His parents laugh because they are happy that he is happy.

ich finde	wir finden
du findest	ihr findet
er, sie, es findet	sie finden

Then they hear an animal. It's a big animal. What kind of animal is it? It's a horse. The horse is slowly going through the forest.

It's a nice horse. High up on the horse a fat woman is sitting. She is happy in the forest.

Hoch oben auf einem Baum sitzt ein Vogel. Der Vogel hat vier Eier. Ein Ei fällt vom Baum. Das Ei fällt auf die Hand der dicken Frau.
Die Frau ruft laut: „Ein Ei!" Sie hat Angst und fällt vom Pferd auf den Boden. Das Pferd rennt schnell durch den Wald.

Herr und Frau Schmidt helfen der dicken Frau. Die Frau steht auf.
„Wie heißen Sie?", fragt Frau Schmidt.
„Ich heiße Müller", sagt die Frau. „Wo ist mein Pferd?"
„Ihr Pferd ist nicht mehr hier", sagt Marie. „Es ist durch den Wald gerannt."
Frau Müller ist unglücklich.
„Das ist sehr schlecht", sagt Frau Müller. „Ich brauche mein Pferd. Ich kann nicht gut zu Fuß gehen, weil ich sehr dick bin."
„Wir werden Ihnen helfen", sagt Herr Schmidt.

ich heiße	wir heißen
du heißt	ihr heißt
er, sie, es heißt	sie heißen

das Pferd ist langsam

High up in a tree a bird is sitting. The bird has four eggs. One egg falls down from the tree. The egg falls onto the hand of the fat woman.

The woman calls loudly "An egg!" She is afraid and falls off the horse onto the ground. The horse runs quickly through the forest.

Mr. and Mrs. Schmidt help the fat woman. The woman stands up.

"What are you called?" Mrs. Schmidt asks.

"I'm called Müller," the woman says. "Where is my horse?"

"Your horse isn't here anymore," Marie says. "It has run through the forest."

Mrs. Müller is unhappy.

"That's very bad," Mrs. Müller says. "I need my horse. I can't walk well because I'm so fat."

"We'll help you," Mr. Schmidt says.

das Ei

Achtes Kapitel

laufen - **go, run**
vor - **before, in front of**
lang - **long**
kurz - **short**

das Bein - **leg**
der Arm - **arm**
böse - **angry, evil**
warten - **wait**

„Sie sehen, dass ich sehr dick bin. Ich kann schlecht zu Fuß gehen. Ich werde auf mein Pferd warten. Mein Pferd muss zu mir kommen."
Die Familie Schmidt und Frau Müller haben lange Zeit gewartet. Das Pferd ist nicht gekommen.
„Ich bin auf meinen Arm gefallen", sagt Frau Müller. „Mein Arm tut mir weh."

mein Arm tut mir weh	**my arm hurts**

Herr Schmidt will nicht mehr warten.
„Wir müssen nach Hause gehen", sagt er zu Frau Müller.
„Kommen Sie mit uns. Ich werde Sie im Auto fahren."
Jetzt geht Frau Müller mit der Familie Schmidt durch den Wald.
Frau Müller sagt immer: „Mein Arm tut mir weh, meine Füße tun mir weh, meine Beine tun mir weh, oh, oh, oh!"
Peter will Frau Müller nicht mehr hören. Er läuft vor zum Auto und wartet auf seine Eltern. Marie läuft ihm nach. Sie will Frau Müller auch nicht mehr hören.

Eighth Chapter

 **der Arm**

"You see that I'm very fat. I'm very bad at walking. I'll wait for my horse. My horse has to come to me."

The Schmidt family and Mrs. Müller waited for a long time. The horse didn't come.
"I fell on my arm," Mrs. Müller says. "My arm hurts."

Mr. Schmidt doesn't want to wait anymore.
"We have to go home," he says to Mrs. Müller. "Come with us. I'll take you in the car."
Now Mrs. Müller is walking with the Schmidt family through the forest.
Mrs. Müller keeps saying "My arm hurts, my feet hurt, my legs hurt, oh, oh, oh!"
Peter doesn't want to hear Mrs. Müller anymore. He runs ahead to the car and waits for his parents. Marie runs after him. She doesn't want to hear Mrs. Müller anymore either.

das Bein

Herr und Frau Schmidt wollen Frau Müller auch nicht mehr hören, aber sie haben gesagt, dass sie ihr helfen werden.
Frau Müller sagt es immer und immer wieder: „Mein Arm! Meine Füße! Meine Beine! Sie tun mir weh!"
Herr Schmidt will auch zu seinem Auto laufen, aber er kann nicht. Er muss Frau Müller helfen.
„Der böse Vogel", sagt Frau Müller sehr laut. „Oh, der böse Vogel. Er hat mir weh getan."
Frau Schmidt will es nicht hören. Langsam wird sie auf Frau Müller böse. „Was sagen Sie da?", fragt sie. „Der Vogel ist nicht böse."
„Der Vogel war sehr böse", sagt Frau Müller sehr laut und sieht Frau Schmidt böse an. „Ich will, dass eine Katze ihn fängt."
Nach kurzer Zeit kommen sie alle zum Auto wo Peter und Marie warten.
„Frau Müller!" rufen die Kinder laut. „Sehen Sie, ihr Pferd ist da."
Es ist richtig. Das große Pferd steht vor dem roten Auto. Das Pferd wartet auf Frau Müller.
Frau Müller ist glücklich, dass sie ihr Pferd hat und die Familie Schmidt ist glücklich, dass Frau Müller nicht mit ihnen im Auto fährt.

der Fuß

Mr. and Mrs. Schmidt don't want to hear Mrs. Müller anymore either, but they said that they would help her.

Mrs. Müller says it over and over again. "My arm! My feet! My legs! They're painful!"

Mr. Schmidt also wants to run to the car, but he can't. He has to help Mrs. Müller.

"That bad bird," Mrs. Müller loudly says. "Oh, that bad bird. It hurt me."

Mrs. Schmidt doesn't want to hear about it. Slowly she is getting annoyed with Mrs. Müller. "What are you talking about?" she asks. "The bird isn't bad."

"The bird was very bad!" Mrs. Müller says very loudly and looks at Mrs. Schmidt angrily. "I want a cat to catch it."

After a short time they all get to the car where Peter and Marie are waiting.

"Mrs. Müller!" the children call loudly. "Look, your horse is here."

It's right. The big horse is standing in front of the red car. The horse is waiting for Mrs. Müller.

Mrs. Müller is happy to have her horse and the Schmidt family are happy that Mrs. Müller isn't coming with them in the car.

Die Familie Schmidt hat Frau Müller geholfen. Und was macht Frau Müller? Sie sagt nichts. Sie nimmt ihr Pferd und geht weg. Das war nicht gut.

„Was für eine böse Frau", sagt Marie. „Ich will sie nicht mehr sehen."

Dann fährt die Familie nach Hause. Fahren sie schnell nach Hause? Nein, sie fahren sehr langsam, weil viele Autos auf der Straße sind.

„Ich fahre gerne", sagt Herr Schmidt, „aber ich habe es nicht gerne, wenn sehr viele Autos auf der Straße sind. Ich will schnell fahren."

„Es war sehr schön im Wald", sagt Frau Schmidt. „Ich gehe immer gerne in den Wald."

„Das ist richtig", sagt Herr Schmidt, „aber Frau Müller will ich nicht mehr sehen und ich will sie auch nicht mehr hören."

Die Kinder singen:

„Dicke böse Müller war auf ihrem Pferd. Es saß ein kleiner Vogel hoch oben in dem Baum. Er hatte viele Eier und eines fiel herab. Es fiel auf ihre Hand und sie fiel auf den Boden. Der Arm der tat ihr weh und sie rief laut ‚Oh je!'"	Bad fat Müller was on her horse. A little bird sat high up in the tree. It had many eggs and one fell down. It fell on her hand and she fell on the ground. Her arm it hurt her so and she cried loud 'Oh no!'

Dann haben die Kinder laut gelacht. Es war nicht lieb von den Kindern so zu singen, man kann auch sagen es war böse.

The Schmidt family have helped Mrs. Müller. And what does Mrs. Müller do? She says nothing. She takes her horse and goes away. That wasn't good.

"What a nasty woman," Marie says. "I don't want to see her again."

Then the family drives home. Are they driving home fast? No, they are driving very slowly because there are many cars on the road.

"I like driving," Mr. Schmidt says, "but I'm not happy when there are so many cars on the road. I want to drive fast."

"It was very nice in the forest," Mrs. Schmidt says. "I'm always happy to go in the forest."

"That's right," Mr. Schmidt says, "but I don't want to see Mrs. Müller again and I don't want to hear her again."

ich will	wir wollen
du willst	ihr wollt
er, sie, es will	sie wollen

Then the children laughed loudly. It wasn't nice of the children to sing like that, one could also say it was nasty.

nur - **only**	bringen - **bring**
andere - **other**	weit - **far**
gleich - **soon**	suchen - **look for**
halten - **hold**	der Schlüssel - **key**

Sie müssen sehr lange im Auto fahren. Sie fahren drei Stunden.

Dann sagt Herr Schmidt: „Wir müssen nur noch kurze Zeit fahren. Es ist nicht mehr weit. Gleich sind wir zu Hause."

Frau Schmidt, Marie und ihr Bruder sind glücklich nach Hause zu kommen. Sie sind sehr lange im Auto gefahren. Sie wollen nicht mehr im Auto sitzen. Sie wollen im Bett liegen und schlafen.

Jetzt sind sie da. Sie machen die Autotüren auf und gehen zum Haus. Die Kinder warten an der Haustür. Sie brauchen den Schlüssel. Die Mutter kommt.

„Wo ist der Schlüssel?", fragt sie.

„Ich habe den Hausschlüssel nicht", sagt ihr Mann.

„Wo ist der Schlüssel?", fragt Frau Schmidt.

„Wir brauchen den Schlüssel", sagen die Kinder. Sie wollen in das Haus gehen, aber sie können es nicht.

Die Eltern suchen den Schlüssel im Auto. Suchen sie den Schlüssel kurze Zeit? Nein, sie suchen den Schlüssel lange Zeit. Sie sind alle unglücklich, weil sie den Schlüssel lange suchen. Sie suchen den Schlüssel eine Stunde lang. Das ist sehr lange und die Kinder sind sehr unglücklich.

„Andere Leute haben ihre Schlüssel", sagt Peter sehr unglücklich. „Andere Leute können ihre Türen aufmachen und in ihre Häuser gehen. Sie können essen und ins Bett gehen. Andere Leute schlafen jetzt."

ich halte	wir halten
du hälst	ihr haltet
er, sie, es hält	sie halten

They have to drive a long time in the car. They drive for three hours.

Then Mr. Schmidt says: "We only have to drive a short time now. It isn't far now. We'll be home soon."

Mrs. Schmidt, Marie and her brother are happy to get home. They were going by car a very long time. They don't want to sit in the car anymore. They want to lie in bed and sleep.

Now they are there. They open the car doors and go to the house. The children are waiting at the front door. They need the key. Mother comes.

"Where's the key?" she asks.

"I haven't got the door key," her husband says.

"Where's the key?" Mrs. Schmidt asks.

"We need the key," the children say. They want to go into the house, but they can't.

The parents look for the key in the car. Are they looking for the key for a short time? No, they are looking for the key for a long time. They are all unhappy because they are looking for the key for a long time. They are looking for the key for one hour. That's very long and the children are very unhappy.

"Other people have their keys," Peter says very unhappily. "Other people can open their doors and go into their houses. They can eat and go to bed. Other people are sleeping now."

der Schlüssel

Jetzt wird Marie böse. „Ich will es nicht mehr hören", sagt sie.
Dann kommt ihr Vater schnell vom Auto zum Haus. In seiner
Hand hält er den Schlüssel. Er bringt den Schlüssel zur Tür.
„Hier ist der Schlüssel", sagt er. „Wir haben lange gesucht,
aber gleich ist die Tür auf. Dann werden wir essen und trinken
und ins Bett gehen."
Nach einer Stunde liegen alle im Bett und schlafen. Ist das
richtig? Nein, es ist nicht richtig. Der Hund liegt nicht im
Bett. Er liegt auf dem Boden und schläft.

 **die Tür**

Now Marie is getting annoyed. "I don't want to hear it anymore," she says. Then father quickly gcomes from the car to the house. He is holding the key in his hand. He is bringing the key to the door.

"Here's the key," he says. "We were looking for a long time but the door will be open in a moment. Then we'll eat and drink and go to bed."

After an hour they're all lying in bed and sleeping. Is that right? No, it isn't right. The dog isn't lying in bed. It's lying on the floor and sleeping.

Neuntes Kapitel

nun - **now**	unten - **down**
fertig - **ready, finished**	bauen - **build**
Onkel - **uncle**	Kopf - **head**
soll - **shall**	Schiff - **ship**

Heute ist Peter glücklich. Er muss nicht in die Schule gehen. Was macht er heute? Er spielt mit seinen Autos und seinen Schiffen, und er baut ein Haus zum Spielen. Wie viele Autos hat er? Er hat sieben Autos. Wie viele Schiffe hat er? Er hat drei Schiffe. Wie viele Häuser baut er? Er baut ein Haus. Peter spielt gerne zu Hause. Spielt er im Garten? Nein, heute spielt er in seinem Zimmer.

das Zimmer - room

„Hallo Peter", sagt seine Schwester. „Was machst du?"
„Ich baue ein Haus und ich spiele mit meinen Autos und Schiffen", sagt er. „Mein Haus ist gleich fertig."
Marie steht vor Peter. In ihrer Hand hält sie ein Stück Brot.
„Ich will nicht mit den Autos und Schiffen spielen", sagt sie. „Ich will das Stück Brot essen. Heute kommt Onkel Thomas zu uns. Du kannst mit ihm spielen."
Peter spielt gerne mit Onkel Thomas. Sein Onkel hat einen großen Kopf und er kann sehr gut spielen.
Die Kinder hören vor dem Haus ein Auto. Sie gehen zum Fenster. Was sehen sie vor dem Haus? Sie sehen ein kleines grünes Auto. Die Tür geht auf. Jetzt sehen sie Onkel Thomas. Ihr Onkel geht zum Haus. In seinen Händen hält er zwei Autos. Er bringt die Autos für Peter und Marie.
Nun macht Herr Schmidt die Haustür auf und sieht seinen Bruder. Onkel Thomas ist der Bruder von Herrn Schmidt.

Ninth Chapter

Today Peter is happy. He doesn't have to go to school.
What is he doing today? He is playing with his cars and his
ships, and he's building a house to play with.
How many cars has he got? He's got seven cars.
How many ships has he got? He's got three ships.
How many houses is he building? He's building one house.
Peter likes playing at home. Is he playing in the garden? No,
today he's playing in his room.

"Hello Peter," his sister says. "What are you doing?"
"I'm building a house and I'm playing with my cars and
ships," he says. "My house will be finished soon."
Marie is standing in front of Peter. She's holding a piece of
bread in her hand. "I don't want to play with cars and ships,"
she says. "I want to eat the piece of bread. Uncle Thomas is
coming to us today. You can play with him."
Peter likes playing with Uncle Thomas. His uncle has got a
big head and he can play very well.
The children hear a car in front of the house. They go to the
window. What do they see in front of the house? They see a
small green car. The door opens. Now they see Uncle
Thomas. Their uncle goes to the house. In his hands he's
holding two cars. He's bringing the cars for Peter and Marie.
Now Mr. Schmidt is opening the front door and he sees his
brother. Uncle Thomas is Mr. Schmidt's brother.

Die beiden Brüder haben sich gerne. Sie geben sich die Hände und lachen.

sie geben sich die Hände	**they shake hands**

Dann sehen die beiden Kinder ihren Onkel. Er gibt Peter ein neues gelbes Auto und er gibt Marie ein neues rotes Auto.
„Danke, Onkel Thomas", sagen die Kinder.
Peter lacht und geht schnell in sein Zimmer. Er will mit dem schönen neuen Auto spielen. Er ist sehr glücklich.
Ist Marie glücklich? Nein, sie ist nicht sehr glücklich. Sie hat Onkel Thomas sehr gerne, aber sie spielt nicht gerne mit Autos. Sie ist nicht glücklich, dass ihr Onkel ihr ein Auto gibt.
Onkel Thomas geht zu Peter ins Zimmer. Er sieht, dass Peter ein Haus baut.
„Soll ich dir helfen das Haus zu bauen?", fragt Onkel Thomas.
„Ja bitte", sagt Peter.
Sein Onkel setzt sich zu ihm auf den Boden. Er hilft Peter das Haus zu bauen. Jetzt ist das Haus fertig. Sie haben es gebaut.
„Was machen wir nun?", fragt Onkel Thomas.
„Jetzt fahren wir mit den Autos zum Haus", sagt Peter. Er gibt seinem Onkel ein weißes Auto und er nimmt das neue gelbe Auto.

 **das Schiff**

Sie spielen für eine Stunde. Dann sagt Onkel Thomas „Ich will jetzt mit deinem Schiff spielen. Soll ich mit dem Schiff zum Haus fahren?"

The two brothers like each other. They shake hands and laugh.

Then the two children see their uncle. He gives Peter a new yellow car and Marie a new red car.
"Thank you, Uncle Thomas," the children say.
Peter is laughing and quickly goes to his room. He wants to play with the nice new car. He's very happy.
Is Marie happy? No, she isn't very happy. She likes Uncle Thomas very much, but she doesn't like playing with cars. She isn't happy that her uncle gives her a car.
Uncle Thomas goes to Peter in his room. He sees that Peter is building a house.
"Shall I help you build the house?" Uncle Thomas asks.

"Yes please," Peter says.
His uncle sits down on the floor with him. He helps Peter to build the house. Now the house is finished. They have built it.
"What are we doing now?" Uncle Thomas asks.
"Now we'll drive the cars to the house," Peter says. He gives his uncle a white car and he takes the new yellow car.

 **zwei Schiffe**

They play for one hour. Then Uncle Thomas says "I want to play with your ship now. Shall I sail the ship to the house?"

Peter gibt seinem Onkel ein blaues Schiff und sagt: „Hier ist dein Schiff."
In Peters Zimmer steht ein kleiner Tisch. Auf dem Tisch sind zwei Autos. Onkel Thomas sitzt auf dem Boden. Da fällt ein Auto vom Tisch auf seinen Kopf. Das tut weh!
„Mein Kopf!", ruft Onkel Thomas laut. „Mein Kopf tut weh. Ein Auto ist auf meinen Kopf gefallen. Ich will nicht mehr spielen."
Onkel Thomas steht auf und geht in die Küche. Er will jetzt essen. Will er Brot essen und Wasser trinken? Nein, er will Kuchen essen und Kaffee trinken.

der Kuchen - **cake**
der Kaffee - **coffee**

Sein Bruder ist nicht da, also macht Thomas den Kaffee für sich selbst. Er trinkt gerne Kaffee. Als der Kaffee fertig ist nimmt er noch ein Stück Kuchen und geht mit Kaffee und Kuchen in den Garten. Da sieht er seinen Bruder.
Wie heißt sein Bruder? Sein Bruder heißt Leo.
Und wie heißt Leos Frau? Sie heißt Lisa.
Leo und Lisa sind ihre Vornamen.
Mit Nachnamen heißen sie Schmidt.
Leo und Lisa sitzen im Garten. Sie essen Kuchen und trinken Kaffee.

schon - **already**   der Opa- **grandad**
lassen - **leave**   die Seite - **side, page**
voll -**full**   schwimmen - **swim**
ganz - **all**

„Hallo Thomas", sagt Lisa. „Bist du schon fertig mit dem Spielen?

Peter gives his uncle a blue ship and says "Here's your ship."

There is a small table standing in Peter's room. There are two cars on the table. Uncle Thomas is sitting on the floor. Then a car falls off the table onto his head. That hurts!
"My head!" Uncle Thomas calls out loud. "My head hurts. A car has fallen on my head. I don't want to play anymore."

Uncle Thomas stands up and goes to the kitchen. He wants to eat now. Does he want to eat bread and drink water? No, he wants to eat cake and drink coffee.

His brother isn't there, so Thomas makes coffee for himself. He likes drinking coffee. When the coffee is ready he also takes a piece of cake and goes with the coffee and cake into the garden. There he sees his brother.
What's his brother called? His brother is called Leo.
And what is Leo's wife called? She is called Lisa.
Leo and Lisa are their first names.
Their family name is Schmidt.
Leo and Lisa are sitting in the garden. They are eating cake and drinking coffee.

"Hello Thomas," Lisa says. Have already finished playing?"

Thomas lacht. „Ja, mir ist ein Auto auf den Kopf gefallen. Jetzt will ich deinen guten Kuchen essen und Kaffee trinken. Ihr habt einen sehr schönen Garten."

Jetzt sitzen die drei im Garten. Kuchen essen, Kaffee trinken und im Garten sitzen mögen sie sehr gerne.

Was macht Marie? Sitzt sie auch im Garten, isst Kuchen und trinkt Kaffee?

Marie sitzt im Garten, aber sie hat nicht Kaffee getrunken, sie hat Wasser getrunken und Kuchen gegessen.

Was macht sie jetzt? Sie sitzt auf dem Boden und liest ein Buch. Sie liest gerne Bücher. Seite für Seite liest sie das Buch. Dann hat sie das ganze Buch gelesen. Was macht sie nun? Sie geht ins Haus, weil sie noch ein Buch holen will. Sie will ein anderes Buch lesen. Sie läßt das alte Buch liegen und nimmt ein neues Buch. Dann kommt sie wieder in den Garten.

 **die Seiten im Buch**

Leo und Lisa haben ihren Kaffee getrunken und den Kuchen gegessen. Thomas ist noch nicht fertig. Er isst sein Stück Kuchen. Seine Tasse Kaffee ist noch voll.

die Tasse - **cup**

Er trinkt den Kaffee langsam. Er will ihn nicht schnell trinken, weil er gerne Kaffee trinkt.

Thomas laughs. "Yes, a car fell on my head.
Now I want to eat your good cake and drink coffee.
You've got a very nice garden."
Now the three are sitting in the garden. Eating cake, drinking
coffee and sitting in the garden are things they like doing.
What is Marie doing? Is she also sitting in the garden, eating
cake and drinking coffee?
Marie is sitting in the garden, but she hasn't drunk any coffee,
she has drunk water and eaten cake.
What is she doing now? She is sitting on the ground and
reading a book. She likes reading books. She's reading the
book page by page. Then she has read the whole book. What
is she doing now? She is going into the house because she
wants to get another book. She wants to read a different book.
She leaves the old book and takes a new book. Then she
comes in the garden again.

viele Bücher

Leo and Lisa have drunk their coffee and eaten the cake.
Thomas hasn't finished yet. He is eating his piece of cake. His
cup of coffee is still full.

He's drinking the coffee slowly. He doesn't want to drink it
quickly because he likes drinking coffee.

Die Sonne scheint, der Himmel ist blau und hoch oben fliegen viele schwarze Vögel.

„Ich sitze sehr gerne bei euch im Garten", sagt Thomas. „Es ist sehr schön hier. Ihr müsst glücklich sein, dass ihr immer hier sitzen könnt."

Leo und Lisa lachen. „Ja, es ist sehr schön im Garten, aber immer können wir hier nicht sitzen," sagen sie.

Da kommt Marie zu ihnen.

„Mamma, Papa", sagt sie, „wo ist Opa heute? Wird Opa auch zu uns kommen?"

„Opa kann heute nicht kommen", sagt Onkel Thomas. „Er ist heute schwimmen gegangen. Er schwimmt sehr gerne."

„Oh", sagt Marie. „Ich will auch schwimmen. Kann ich schwimmen gehen?"

Vater und Mutter sehen sich an.

„Ja", sagen sie, „wir wollen auch schwimmen gehen. Wir werden in einer Stunde schwimmen gehen."

„Und was ist mit dir, Thomas?", fragt Leo. „Willst du auch schwimmen gehen?"

„Nein Danke", sagt Thomas. „Ich kann heute nicht schwimmen gehen. Ich muss nach Hause fahren. Es ist immer sehr schön bei euch, aber ich habe nicht mehr viel Zeit."

 **das Mädchen schwimmt im Wasser**

The sun is shining, the sky is blue and high up many black birds are flying.

"I like sitting with you in your garden," Thomas says. "It's always nice here. You must be happy that you can always sit here."

Leo and Lisa laugh. "Yes, it's very nice in the garden, but we can't always sit here," they say.

Marie comes to them.

"Mama, papa," she says, "where's grandad today? Is grandad also coming?"

"Grandad can't come today," Uncle Thomas says. "He's gone swimming today. He likes swimming very much."

"Oh," Marie says. "I also want to swim. Can I go swimming?"

Father and mother look at one another.

"Yes," they say, "we also want to go swimming. We'll go swimming in an hour."

"And what about you, Thomas?" Leo asks. "Do you also want to go swimming?"

"No thanks," Thomas says. "I can't go swimming today. I have to drive home. It's always very nice with you, but I haven't got much time left."

Zehntes Kapitel

Lieber Leser!
Was haben Sie in diesem Buch schon gelesen? Sie haben von der Familie Schmidt gelesen. In dieser Familie gibt es vier Leute und ein Tier. Da ist ein Mann, Herr Schmidt, und seine Frau. Frau Schmidt heißt mit Vornamen Lisa und ihr Mann heißt Leo. Die beiden haben zwei Kinder. Ein Kind ist ein Mädchen und heißt Marie. Das andere Kind ist ein Junge und heißt Peter. Marie ist die Schwester von Peter und er ist ihr Bruder. Es gibt auch ein Tier in der Familie, einen Hund der Rex heißt. Der Nachname der Familie ist Schmidt.
Die Familie hat ein Haus mit einem schönen Garten in dem es Blumen und Bäume gibt. Im Garten können sie Vögel sehen. Die Vögel fliegen, aber die Leute und der Hund gehen zu Fuß. Die Familie ist nicht immer zu Hause. Herr Schmidt muss in die Stadt fahren, wo er arbeitet. Er arbeitet acht Stunden am Tag. Er fährt nicht gerne in die Stadt, aber seine Frau geht gerne in die Stadt zum Einkaufen.

Einkaufen - **shopping**

Gehen Sie, lieber Leser, auch gerne Einkaufen?
Die Kinder gehen zu Fuß in die Schule. Peter hat in der Schule ein Buch gelesen und Marie hat gearbeitet und geschrieben. Sie waren fünf Stunden in der Schule. Die beiden Kinder sind gerne zu Hause. Da spielen sie mit Autos und Schiffen, und mit einem Ball und Rex im Garten. Sie spielen aber nicht auf der Straße, weil sie da Angst haben.
Eines Tages war ihr Onkel Thomas bei ihnen. Er hat ihnen neue Autos zum Spielen gegeben. Peter war glücklich, aber Marie spielt nicht gerne mit Autos.
Einmal ist die Familie in den Wald gefahren. Es war sehr schön im Wald. Was haben sie gemacht?

Tenth Chapter

Dear Reader,
What have you already read in this book? You have read about the Schmidt family. In this family there are four people and one animal. There is a man, Mr. Schmidt, and his wife. Mrs. Schmidt's first name is Lisa and her husband is called Leo. They have two children. One child is a girl and is called Marie. The other child is a boy and is called Peter. Marie is Peter's sister and he is her brother.
There is also an animal in the family, a dog called Rex. Their family name is Schmidt.
The family have a house with a nice garden in which there are flowers and trees. They can see birds in the garden. The birds fly but the people and the dog go on foot.
The family isn't always at home. Mr. Schmidt has to go into town where he works. He works eight hours a day. He doesn't like going into town, but his wife likes going into town to go shopping.

Do you, dear Reader, also like to go shopping?
The children go to school on foot. Peter read a book at school and Marie worked and wrote. They were at school for five hours. The two children like being at home. There they play with cars and ships, and with a ball and Rex in the garden. But they don't play on the road because they are afraid there.
One day Uncle Thomas was with them. He gave them new cars to play with. Peter was happy, but Marie doesn't like playing with cars.

One day the family drove to a forest. It was very nice in the forest. What did they do?

Herr und Frau Schmidt sind Hand in Hand durch den Wald gegangen. Peter ist gerannt und Marie hat sich auf einen großen Stein gesetzt wo sie gesungen hat. Sie hat eine weiße Katze gesehen die eine kleine Maus gefangen hat.

Dann hat ihre Mutter sie gerufen und sie ist zu ihr gekommen. Dann haben sie ein großes Tier gehört. Es war ein Pferd und auf dem Pferd saß eine sehr dicke Frau. Ein Ei ist von einem Baum auf die Frau gefallen und die dicke Frau ist vom Pferd auf den Boden gefallen und hat sich weh getan. Das war schlecht. Ihr Pferd ist durch den Wald gerannt.

Die Frau hat gesagt, dass sie Müller heißt. Die Familie Schmidt wollte ihr helfen und sie mit dem Auto nach Hause fahren, aber Frau Müller wollte auf ihr Pferd warten. Das Pferd ist nicht mehr gekommen. Dann ist Frau Müller doch mit der Familie Schmidt durch den Wald gegangen. Was hat Frau Müller gesagt?

„Mein Arm tut mir weh, meine Beine tun mir weh, meine Füße tun mir weh!"

Sie hat es immer und immer wieder gesagt. Die Kinder wollten sie nicht mehr hören.

Dann sind sie zu Herrn Schmidts Auto gekommen. Da stand das Pferd von Frau Müller.

Im Auto haben die Kinder ein böses Lied gesungen.

das Lied - **song**

Das war nicht lieb.

Sie sind lange und sehr langsam nach Hause gefahren. Dann haben sie eine Stunde lang den Hausschlüssel gesucht. Das war schlecht.

Und was hat die Familie Schmidt nach dem Besuch von Onkel Thomas gemacht?

der Besuch - **visit**

Mr. and Mrs. Schmidt walked hand in hand through the forest. Peter went running and Marie sat on a big stone where she was singing. She saw a white cat that caught a little mouse.

Then her mother called her and she came to her.
Then they heard a large animal. It was a horse and on the horse there was a very fat woman. An egg fell down from a tree onto the fat woman and the fat woman fell off the horse onto the ground and hurt herself. That was bad. Her horse ran through the forest.
The woman said that she was called Müller. The Schmidt family wanted to help her and drive her home in the car, but Mrs. Müller wanted to wait for her horse. The horse didn't come again. Then Mrs. Müller went with the Schmidt family through the forest after all. What did Mrs. Müller say?

"My arm hurts, my legs hurt, my feet hurt!"

She said it over and over again. The children didn't want to hear her anymore.
Then they reached Mr. Schmidt's car. Mrs. Müller's horse was standing there.
In the car the children sang a nasty song.

That wasn't nice.
They drove home for a long time and very slowly. Then they looked for the front door key for an hour. That was bad.

And what did the Schmidt family do after Uncle Thomas's visit?

Wie der Opa von Marie und Peter sind sie schwimmen gegangen. Sie gehen immer gerne schwimmen.
Und was ist mit Ihnen, lieber Leser? Gehen Sie auch gerne schwimmen?

eine Tasse Kaffee

Just like Marie and Peter's grandad they went swimming. They always like to go swimming.
And what about you, dear Reader? Do you like to go swimming?

Spielzeugautos – toy cars

Elftes Kapitel

Opa schwimmt gerne. Er schwimmt jetzt schon zwei Stunden. Ist seine Frau bei ihm? Nein, er hat sie zu Hause gelassen. Opa schwimmt von einer Seite des Beckens zur anderen.

das Becken - pool

Das Becken ist voll Wasser. Opa ist ganz im Wasser, nur sein Kopf ist über dem Wasser.

über - above

„Jetzt bin ich gleich fertig mit dem Schwimmen", denkt Opa. „Was soll ich nach dem Schwimmen machen? Soll ich gleich nach Hause gehen oder soll ich noch ein Stück Kuchen essen und eine Tasse Kaffee trinken gehen?"
Opa will nicht nach Hause gehen, also geht er in ein Café. Warum will er nicht nach Hause gehen? Er will die Fragen seiner Frau nicht hören.
„Wo warst du? Warum bist du schwimmen gegangen? Warum warst du so lange schwimmen? Wo warst du nach dem Schwimmen? Wer ist mit dir geschwommen?"
Diese und viele andere Fragen hört Opa immer von seiner Frau. Also geht er in ein Café. Er trinkt eine gute Tasse Kaffee und isst ein Stück Kuchen. Dann sucht er sein Geld. Er braucht das Geld um den Kuchen und den Kaffee zu bezahlen.

bezahlen - pay for

Wo ist sein Geld? Er sucht und sucht aber er findet es nicht.

Eleventh Chapter

Grandad likes swimming. He's been swimming for two hours.
Is his wife with him? No, he's left her at home.
Grandad is swimming from one side of the pool to the other.

das Schwimmbecken - **swimming pool**

The pool is full of water. Grandad is fully in the water, only
his head is above the water.

"I've almost finished swimming," grandad thinks. "What shall
I do after swimming? Shall I go straight home or shall I go to
eat a piece of cake and drink a cup of coffee?"

Grandad doesn't want to go home, so he goes to a cafe.
Why doesn't he want to go home? He doesn't want to hear his
wife's questions.
"Where have you been? Why did you go swimming? Why
were you swimming for so long? Where were you after you
were swimming? Who was swimming with you?"
These and many other questions grandad always hears from
his wife. So he goes to a cafe. He drinks a good cup of coffee
and eats a piece of cake. Then he looks for his money. He
needs the money to pay for the cake and the coffee.

Where is his money? He keeps looking but he can't find it.

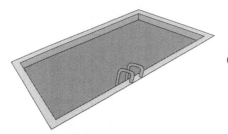

das Schwimmbecken

„O je", sagt Opa. „Ich habe mein Geld am Becken liegen gelassen. Ich muss wieder zum Becken gehen und mein Geld holen."
Jetzt ist der Mann im Café böse auf Opa.
„Warum haben Sie kein Geld?", fragt der Mann.

kein Geld - **no money**

„Sie haben Kuchen gegessen und Kaffee getrunken. Sie müssen bezahlen!"
„Ich war beim Schwimmen und habe mein Geld dort liegen gelassen", sagt Opa. „Ich muss mein Geld holen. Dann kann ich für Kaffee und Kuchen bezahlen."
Jetzt wird der Mann im Café rot im Gesicht.

das Gesicht - **face**

„Ha!", sagt der Mann. „Sie wollen nicht bezahlen. Sie wollen nur weglaufen."
Jetzt wird Opa rot im Gesicht.
„Ich laufe nicht weg", sagt er und sieht den Mann böse an.
„Ich bezahle immer", ruft Opa laut.
Jetzt ruft der Mann auch laut.
Alle Leute im Café sehen zu Opa und dem Mann. Da geht die Tür zum Café auf. Wer kommt in das Café?

ein Kuchen

"Oh dear," grandad says. "I've left my money lying by the pool. I have to go to the pool again and fetch my money."

Now the man in the cafe is cross with grandad.
"Why haven't you got any money?" the man asks.

"You've eaten cake and drunk coffee. You have to pay!"

"I was swimming and I left my money lying there," grandad says. "I have to fetch my money. Then I can pay for the coffee and cake."
Now the man in the cafe becomes red in the face.

"Ha!" the man says. "You don't want to pay. You just want to run away."
Now grandad is going red in the face.
"I'm not running away," he says and looks at the man angrily.
"I always pay," grandad calls loudly.
Now the man is also calling loudly.
All the people in the cafe are looking to grandad and the man.
The cafe door opens. Who is coming into the cafe?

Opas Frau kommt in das Café. Opa ist sehr glücklich seine Frau zu sehen.

„Ich habe mein Geld nach dem Schwimmen liegen gelassen", ruft Opa laut zu seiner Frau. „Aber dieser böse Mann sagt, dass ich nicht bezahlen will. Er sagt, dass ich weglaufen will."

die Oma - **grandma**

Oma hat viel Geld. Sie bezahlt schnell für ihren Mann. Dann gehen die beiden aus dem Café.

„Danke!", sagt Opa zu seiner Frau. „Ich bin sehr glücklich, dass du gekommen bist und mir geholfen hast."

Oma lacht. Sie nimmt seine Hand und sie gehen nach Hause. Oma liebt ihren Mann und ihr Mann liebt sie.

Als sie zu Hause sind nimmt Oma ihren Schlüssel und öffnet die Haustür. Sie gehen in ihr Haus und ziehen die Schuhe aus.

ausziehen - **take off** (clothes, shoes)

Oma geht in die Küche und sagt: „Komm mit mir. Warum bist du in ein Café gegangen? Ich habe einen Kuchen gemacht, als du beim Schwimmen warst und jetzt werde ich Kaffee machen. Dann können wir hier Kuchen essen und Kaffee trinken. Und du musst keine Angst haben, dass du bezahlen musst. Ich will kein Geld von dir."

Oma hat ihren Mann glücklich gemacht.

„Zu Hause", sagt Opa, „ ist es doch am schönsten."

schön	schöner	am schönsten
nice	nicer	the nicest

Grandad's wife comes into the cafe. Grandad is very happy to see his wife.

"I left my money lying after I was swimming," he calls loudly to his wife. "But this nasty man says that I don't want to pay. He says that I want to run away."

Grandma has a lot of money. She quickly pays for her husband. Then they both leave the cafe.

"Thanks!" grandad says to his wife. "I'm really glad that you came and helped me."

Grandma laughs. She takes his hand and they go home.

Grandma loves her husband and he loves her.

When they are at their home grandma takes her key and opens the front door. They go into the house and take their shoes off.

Grandma goes into the kitchen and says "Come with me. Why did you go to a cafe? I made a cake while you were swimming and now I'll make coffee. Then we can eat cake here and drink coffee. And you don't have to worry that you have to pay. I don't want any money from you."

Grandma has made her husband very happy.

"At home," grandad says, "it's nicest after all."

Zwölftes Kapitel

ich habe gegessen	wir haben gegessen
du hast gegessen	ihr habt gegessen
er, sie, es hat gegessen	sie haben gegessen

essen - gegessen
fangen - gefangen
stellen - gestellt
bauen - gebaut
finden - gefunden
fragen - gefragt
können - gekonnt
kaufen - gekauft
rufen - gerufen
sagen - gesagt
suchen - gesucht
tragen - getragen
trinken - getrunken
tun - getan
bekommen - bekommen
geben - gegeben
haben - gehabt
halten - gehalten
lachen - gelacht
lassen - gelassen
legen - gelegt

lesen - gelesen
schlafen - geschlafen
schreiben - geschrieben
brauchen - gebraucht
bringen - gebracht
denken - gedacht
helfen - geholfen
machen - gemacht
sehen - gesehen
setzen - gesetzt
warten - gewartet
dürfen - gedurft
erzählen - erzählt
holen - geholt
hören - gehört
nehmen - genommen
singen - gesungen
spielen - gespielt
sprechen - gesprochen
wollen - gewollt
weinen - geweint

Twelfth Chapter

There is a past simple form of verbs in German but this is mainly used in formal and literary language.

To express a past action in everyday German it is common to use a form of the auxiliary verb 'haben' or 'sein' and the past participle.

You have seen all these forms in earlier chapters, but now we are going to take a closer look at the two groups separately. In this chapter we'll be dealing with verbs that take the auxiliary 'haben' and in the next chapter you will see all the verbs that go with the auxiliary 'sein'.

By now you may be thinking, hold on, I didn't buy a grammar book. I just wanted an easy reader. And that's exactly what you are getting. By putting the verbs in two different texts it will be easier for you to form correct sentences in the past.

So relax, read the text and you will learn as you read.

Gestern - **yesterday**

Gestern war die Familie Schmidt bei Oma und Opa zu Besuch. Was haben sie alle gemacht?
Opa hat Peter ein neues Schiff gegeben. Hat Peter gleich damit gespielt? Nein, er hat das Schiff gebaut und dann hat er damit gespielt.
Oma hat Marie eine schöne Geschichte erzählt. Hat Marie diese Geschichte schon gehört? Nein, es war eine neue Geschichte für sie. Hat Oma Marie nichts gegeben? Doch, sie hat ihr eine Stück Kuchen gegeben.
Leo und Lisa haben eine Flasche Wein gebracht.

eine Flasche Wein - **a bottle of wine**

Oma und Opa haben die Flasche Wein genommen. Dann haben sie gelacht und Oma hat gesagt: „Vielen Dank, wir trinken gerne Wein."
Haben sie den Wein getrunken? Ja, sie haben alle Wein getrunken. Ist das richtig? Haben die Kinder Wein getrunken? Nein, nur ihre Eltern und Oma und Opa haben Wein getrunken.
Wo waren sie als sie den Wein getrunken haben? Sie waren im Wohnzimmer.

das Wohnzimmer - **living room**
leer - **empty**

Sie haben sich auf das Sofa gesetzt und sie haben dort den Wein getrunken. Nach einer Stunde war die Flasche Wein nicht mehr voll. Sie war leer.
Dann hat Opa noch eine Flasche Wein aus der Küche geholt. Sie waren glücklich und haben den Wein langsam getrunken.

Yesterday the Schmidt family paid grandma and grandad a visit. What did they all do?
Grandad gave Peter a new ship. Did Peter play with it at once? No, he built the ship and then he played with it.

Grandma told Marie a nice story. Had Marie already heard the story? No, it was a new story for her. Didn't grandma give Marie anything? Yes, she gave her a piece of cake.

Leo and Lisa brought a bottle of wine.

Grandma and grandad took the bottle of wine. Then they laughed and grandma said "Thanks a lot, we like drinking wine."
Did they drink the wine? Yes, they all drank wine. Is that right? Did the children drink wine? No, only their parents and grandma and grandad drank wine.

Where were they when they were drinking wine? They were in the living room.

They sat on the sofa and drank the wine there. After an hour the bottle of wine wasn't full anymore. It was empty.

Then grandad got another bottle of wine from the kitchen. They were happy and drank the wine slowly.

Die Kinder haben im Garten „Fangen" gespielt. Peter hat Marie immer gefangen. Dann hat Marie nicht mehr gewollt und hat gesagt: „Ich will nicht mehr mit dir spielen." Sie hat Peter allein gelassen und hat ein Buch gelesen. Peter hat geweint und er hat seine Schwester gerufen, aber sie hat ihn nicht gehört. Wer hat Peter gehört? Opa hat ihn gehört und hat ihm das neue Schiff zum Spielen in den Garten gebracht. Als Peter das Schiff gesehen hat war er wieder glücklich. Er hat nicht mehr geweint, er hat gelacht. Hat Marie auch gelacht? Nein, sie hat nicht gelacht, sie hat ihr Buch gelesen. Als sie das ganze Buch fertig gelesen hat, hat sie es auf einen Tisch gelegt und hat ein Lied gesungen. Peter hat gehört wie seine Schwester gesungen hat. Haben Peter und Opa auch gesungen? Nein, sie haben mehr Schiffe geholt und sie haben gespielt.
Oma und Lisa waren in der Küche und haben das Essen gemacht. Wer hat ihnen geholfen?

niemand - **nobody**

Niemand hat ihnen geholfen. Sie haben das Essen alleine gemacht.
Wer hat mit Marie gesungen? Niemand hat mit ihr gesungen. Sie hat alleine gesungen.
Als das Essen fertig war haben sie es auf den Tisch gestellt. Was haben sie noch auf den Tisch gestellt? Sie haben Wasser und Kaffee auf den Tisch gestellt.
Dann hat Lisa die anderen gerufen und sie haben sich alle an den Tisch gesetzt. Sie haben gegessen und getrunken.
Oma hat eine Tasse Kaffee in der Hand gehalten und sie hat gesagt: „Ich trinke gerne Kaffee. Ich habe schon lange keinen Kaffee mehr getrunken."

The children were playing 'catch me' in the garden. Peter always caught Marie. Then Marie didn't want to anymore and said "I don't want to play with you anymore." She left Peter alone and read a book.

Peter cried and he called his sister, but she didn't hear him.

Who heard Peter? Grandad heard him and brought him the new ship to the garden to play with. When Peter saw the ship he was happy again.

He didn't cry anymore, he laughed. Did Marie laugh too?

No, she didn't laugh, she was reading her book.

When she finished reading the book, she put it on a table and sang a song. Peter heard his sister sing.

Did Peter and grandad also sing?

No, they got more ships and they played.

Grandma and Lisa were in the kitchen and made the food. Who helped them?

Nobody helped them. They prepared the food on their own.

Who was singing with Marie? Nobody sang with her. She was singing on her own.

When the food was ready they put it on the table.

What else did they put on the table? They put water and coffee on the table.

Then Lisa called the others and they all sat down at the table. They ate and drank.

Grandma was holding a cup of coffee in her hand and she said "I like drinking coffee. I haven't drunk coffee for a long time."

109

Beim Essen haben sie alle miteinander gesprochen. Nur Marie hat nichts gesagt. „Warum sprichst du nicht mit uns?", hat ihre Mutter sie gefragt.

„Ich habe über etwas nachgedacht", hat Marie gesagt.

etwas - **something**

„Und über was hast du nachgedacht?", hat ihre Mutter gefragt.

„Ich habe heute ein Buch gesucht und ich habe darüber nachgedacht, wo es ist."

„Hast du das Buch nicht gefunden?"

„Nein, ich habe es nicht gefunden. Ich habe in allen Zimmern gesucht, aber ich habe es nicht gefunden."

„Hast du es zu Hause gelassen?"

„Nein, ich habe es zu Oma und Opa gebracht."

"Hast du sie gefragt, ob sie es gesehen haben?"

ob - **if**

„Nein, ich habe sie nicht gefragt."

Marie hat dann Oma und Opa gefragt: „Habt ihr mein Buch gesehen?"

„Wo hast du das Buch gelassen?"

„Ich habe es auf dem Tisch gelassen. Peter hat mich im Garten immer gefangen. Dann habe ich das Buch gelesen and dann habe ich es auf den Tisch gelegt."

„Ja", hat Oma gesagt. „Ich habe das Buch gefunden und ich habe es im Wohnzimmer auf den Boden gelegt. Ich habe den Tisch für unser Essen gebraucht."

Dann war Marie wieder glücklich.

„Und was ist mit dir, Leo? Was hast du gemacht?", hat seine Frau ihn gefragt.

„Ich habe einen Brief geschrieben."

110

During the meal they were all talking with one another. Only Marie didn't say anything. "Why aren't you talking with us?" her mother asked.

"I was thinking about something," Marie said.

"And what were you thinking about?" her mother asked.

"I was looking for a book today and I was thinking about where it is."

"Didn't you find the book?"

"No, I haven't found it. I looked in all the rooms, but I didn't find it."

"Did you leave it at home?"

"No, I brought it to grandma and grandad's"

"Have you asked them if they have seen it?"

"No, I haven't asked them."

Then Marie asked grandma and grandad: "Have you seen my book?"

"Where did you leave the book?"

"I left it on the table. Peter kept catching me in the garden. Then I read a book and then I put it on the table."

"Yes," grandma said. "I found the book and I put it on the floor in the living room. I needed the table for our meal."

Then Marie was happy again.

"And what about you, Leo? What did you do?" his wife asked him.

"I wrote a letter."

der Brief - **a letter**

„Warum hast du einen Brief geschrieben?"
„Ein Freund hat mir geholfen. Er hat lange auf mich gewartet und er hat viel für mich getan. Ich habe den Brief geschrieben um ihm „Danke" zu sagen."
Dann hat Oma gesehen, dass sie alles gegessen und getrunken haben. Sie hat das Geschirr in die Küche getragen und Marie und Lisa haben ihr geholfen.

das Geschirr - **dishes, crockery**

das schöne weiße Geschirr

| ich schreibe einen Brief | **I am writing a letter** |

"Why did you write a letter?"
"A friend helped me. He waited for me for a long time and he did a lot for me. I wrote the letter to say 'Thank you'."

Then grandma saw that they had eaten and drunk everything. She carried the dishes into the kitchen and Marie and Lisa helped her.

eine Flasche Wein

Dreizehntes Kapitel

ich bin gefahren	wir sind gefahren
du bist gefahren	ihr seid gefahren
er, sie, es ist gefahren	sie sind gefahren

fahren - gefahren
fallen - gefallen
stehen - gestanden
fliegen - geflogen
kommen - gekommen
rennen - gerannt
schwimmen - geschwommen

liegen - gelegen
gehen - gegangen
laufen - gelaufen
sitzen - gesessen
springen - gesprungen

letzte Woche - **last week**

Und was war letzte Woche? Die Familie Schmidt ist letzte
Woche in den Wald gefahren. Peter ist im Wald gerannt aber
er ist nicht gefallen. Ist Marie mit ihm gerannt? Nein, sie ist
nicht gerannt. Sie ist langsam durch den Wald gegangen. Sie
ist auf einem großen Stein gesessen. Viele Vögel sind durch
den Wald geflogen. Dann ist eine kleine schwarze Maus
gekommen. Sie ist nicht gerannt, sie ist langsam gegangen.
Aber dann ist eine weiße Katze gekommen. Die Katze ist
gerannt und dann ist sie auf die Maus gesprungen.
Ist Marie vom Stein gefallen? Nein, sie ist vom Stein
gesprungen.
Da war auch ein kleiner See im Wald.

der See - **lake**

Thirteenth Chapter

In this chapter we will practise the verbs that take the auxiliary 'sein'. This is also a useful revision of all the verbs you have read in this book.

ein kleiner See im Wald

And what was last week? The Schmidt family drove to a forest last week. Peter was running in the forest but he didn't fall. Did Marie run with him? No, she didn't run.
She slowly walked through the forest. She was sitting on a big stone. Many birds were flying through the forest.
Then a little black mouse came.
It didn't run, it walked slowly.
But then a white cat came. The cat ran and jumped on the mouse.
Did Marie fall off the stone? No, she jumped off the stone.

There was also a little lake in the forest.

Peter ist vor dem See gestanden. Ist er auch im See geschwommen? Nein, er ist nicht ins Wasser gegangen und er ist nicht geschwommen.

Aber es ist eine dicke Frau auf einem Pferd gekommen. Ein Ei ist auf die Frau gefallen und die Frau ist auf den Boden gefallen.

Die Frau ist auf dem Boden gelegen. Ist sie lange auf dem Boden gelegen? Nein, sie ist schnell aufgestanden.

aufstehen - stand up

Ist die dicke Frau dann durch den Wald gelaufen? Nein, ihr Pferd ist durch den Wald gelaufen. Die Frau ist langsam durch den Wald gegangen.

Am Abend ist die Familie Schmidt nach Hause gefahren. Sie sind lange im Auto gesessen. Warum sind sie lange gesessen? Weil sehr viele Autos auf der Straße waren und Herr Schmidt sehr langsam gefahren ist.

ankommen - arrive

Als sie angekommen sind waren die Kinder sehr glücklich und sind gesprungen. Aber dann sind sie lange vor dem Haus gestanden, weil niemand den Türschlüssel hatte.

Als sie wieder im Haus waren sind sie alle in ihre Betten gefallen.

Ist Onkel Thomas mit ihnen in den Wald gekommen? Nein, er ist in die Stadt gefahren. Dort ist er mit einer Freundin in ein Café gegangen. Sie sind drei Stunden im Café gesessen.

Oma und Opa sind letzte Woche durch die Stadt gelaufen. Sie sind mit einem Bus gekommen. Sie sind lange gestanden, aber sie sind nicht gerannt und auch nicht gesprungen. Das können sie nicht mehr, weil sie alt sind.

Peter was standing in front of the lake. Did he swim in the lake? No, he didn't go in the water and he didn't swim.

But a fat woman on a horse came. An egg fell on the woman and the woman fell to the ground.

The woman was lying on the ground. Was she lying long on the ground? No, she stood up quickly.

ich stehe auf	**I stand up**

Did the fat woman run through the forest? No, her horse ran through the forest. The woman walked slowly through the forest.

In the evening the Schmidt family drove home. They were sitting in the car a long time. Why did they sit a long time? Because there were many cars on the road and Mr. Schmidt drove slowly.

ich komme an	**I arrive**

When they arrived the children were very happy and jumped. But then they stood a long time in front of the house because nobody had the key to the front door.

When they were in the house again they all dropped into their beds.

Did Uncle Thomas come with them to the forest? No, he went into town. There he went into a cafe with a female friend. They were sitting in a cafe for three hours.

Grandma and grandad walked through town last week. They came by bus. They were standing a long time but they didn't run and they also didn't jump. They can't do so anymore because they are old.

This book is an independent effort. Thank you for supporting free authors. Should you find a mistake or have any suggestions or comments please contact the author at:

books@briansmith.de

www.briansmith.de

By the same author

Super 1000 German Pre-intermediate Reader

German Intermediate Readers:

- Excitement in Munich

- Winter Wonderland

- Bliss in Bavaria

www.briansmith.de

Made in the USA
San Bernardino, CA
24 May 2017